CW00751570

PENGUIN B(

THE STORIES WOMEN JOURNALISTS TELL

Reta Lee is currently working as an editor-in-chief for an online media brand and has previously written for many Malaysian, Singaporean and International publications.

Reta's first foray in publishing began in 2006 after university, when she was writing for two entertainment magazines, *Hot Potato* and *HELLO!* in Malaysia, covering both lifestyle and entertainment beats (both magazines have since ceased). Then, she rode the digital wave 2009 onwards, when she wrote for *MSN Malaysia* and *Business Insider*. As an entertainment journalist by heart—she's interviewed everyone from Lady Gaga, to James Marsden, Sophie Turner, and Susan Downey.

When not writing, she has found time to moderate panel sessions at the previous Millennial 20/20 Summit in 2016 and 2017, and Fashion Tech Summit as part of Singapore Fashion Week in 2017. She also loves catching up on drama series, practising yoga, reading, travelling the world and dabbling in analog photography. She lives in Singapore with her husband Benjamin and their two cats.

The Stories Women Journalists Tell

edited by Reta Lee

PENGUIN BOOKS

An imprint of Penguin Random House

PENGUIN BOOKS

USA | Canada | UK | Ireland | Australia
New Zealand | India | South Africa | China | Southeast Asia

Penguin Books is part of the Penguin Random House group of companies
whose addresses can be found at global.penguinrandomhouse.com

Published by Penguin Random House SEA Pte Ltd
9, Changi South Street 3, Level 08-01,
Singapore 486361

First published in Penguin Books by Penguin Random House SEA 2021
Copyright © Reta Lee 2021

ISBN 978-9-8149-1443-7

Typeset in Adobe Garamond Pro by MAP Systems, Bangalore, India
Printed at Markono Print Media Pte Ltd, Singapore

www.penguin.sg

Contents

Preface

By Reta Lee

I was never trained in hard news reporting. My first foray in writing began in 2006, when I was writing for entertainment magazines, *hot* and *HELLO!* in Malaysia, covering both lifestyle and entertainment beats (both the magazines have since ceased). Then, I rode the digital wave in 2009, when I was writing for *msn.com.my* and haven't looked back since. I'm currently a chief editor for an online media brand, and I couldn't imagine a day without content writing!

I stumbled into politics when my country, Malaysia, was facing a political upheaval in 2011 as thousands of citizens marched for a clean electoral reform and a change in government.

Together with my fellow Malaysians, I marched and reported on the Bersih 2.0 and 3.0 rallies in the heart of Kuala Lumpur. Back then, the reports were for *msn.com.my*. I was the only female writer on my team to contribute the stories on the rallies, which went down in history as one of the historical news events to blow up in Southeast Asia.

Journalism and trusted news reporting calls for professional production of quality, original content, developed by obtaining information from reliable sources through a transparent process. We have a civic duty to our readers to inform and educate, which means an editorial team is often racing against the clock to ensure we deliver credible, unbiased content that people can trust and rely on.

As a female writer, I sought out other fellow female journalists for kinship. The number of women in media professions may have increased in recent years, but there is still a gender imbalance and lack of diversity in newsrooms, film sets, and so forth.

In the International Women's Media Foundation's 2011 Global Report on the Status of Women in News Media, covering over 500 media companies in nearly sixty countries, it was revealed that in most parts of the world women continue to be under-represented as professionals working in both print and broadcast media.[1]

In Asia, only twenty per cent of news subjects were female; the corresponding figure for the Pacific region was twenty-five per cent.[2] The Global Media Monitoring Project 2010 survey found that only twenty-two per cent of the people heard or read about in the news in India was female; the corresponding figures for Malaysia and Nepal were the same: fifteen per cent.[3] Although women's presence in the news had improved by six per cent in Latin America and five per cent in Europe between 2005 and 2010, other regions had either stagnated or registered minimal gains.[4]

I was drawn to the idea of collecting stories from other female journalists who have been on the ground reporting and seeing things from a different perspective. I believe *The Stories Female Journalists Tell* will appeal to all readers regardless of age, race, and gender, who want to broaden their minds about news reporting. I hope their stories will touch and inspire you, wherever you're reading this in the world.

Footnotes

[1]International Women's Media Foundation (IWMF) 2011, Global Report on the Status of Women in News Media, Washington: IWMF. http://www.iwmf.org/wp-content/uploads/2013/09/IWMF-Global-Report-Summary.pdf

[2]The countries included in the Global Media Monitoring Project (GMMP) 2010 survey in Asia were: Bangladesh, China, India, Japan, Kyrgyzstan, Malaysia, Nepal, Pakistan, The Philippines, South Korea, Taiwan, Thailand and Vietnam. The countries included in the GMMP 2010 survey in the Pacific were: Australia, Fiji, New Zealand, Papua New Guinea and Tonga. Four of the Asian countries—India, Malaysia,

Nepal and Pakistan—are included in the present research on media and gender in Asia and the Pacific. Since the Asia regional report was not available on the GMMP website, these figures have been sourced from the global report.

[3]The Pakistan country report was not available on the GMMP website.

[4]The regional and national reports of the GMMP 2010 are available here: http://whomakesthenews.org/gmmp/gmmpreports/gmmp-2010-reports; the Asia regional report and the Pakistan country report were not available on the website in October 2014 or February 2015.

Of Daring, Death and Durian

By Seema Viswanathan

'Where will you pee?'

'Guys can piss anywhere. There are no proper toilets there and you girls will have problems.'

'Really, now,' I thought. After answering the numerous doubts, about why we, two women, my colleague and senior reporter, the late Claudia Theophilus and I, couldn't, shouldn't, mustn't be sent to inner Perak to stake out a military operation centred in a dusun durian, which means durian orchard in the Malay language, this was the last 'difficulty' they had to throw at us.

'Where would we pee?' we exclaimed simultaneously. 'In a bottle? On the roadside? In some bushes? Why the fuck do you care where we will pee?' we asked. I should add, that last question was asked in our heads, but the sentiment showed on our faces.

'They', being the news desk editors, thought enlightening us of a few minor inconveniences would deter us from wanting to be assigned to what was the biggest story gripping the nation that year.

This was July 2000, a few days after a group of 'terrorists' (and I put that in quote marks because, at the time, nobody was entirely sure who these people were) had pulled off an arms heist from two military camps in the state of Perak. What mystery! I loved mysteries. They present the opportunity to explore, probe, investigate, discover, all of which, being a young reporter, would feed my need for adventure.

To make things even more dramatic and exciting, in my eye at least, the group had taken off for the hills, quite literally, near the one-street town of Sauk in the state of Perak along Route 76, the trunk road between Kuala Kangsar and Gerik, following which they kidnapped two policemen. They would eventually also hold hostage an army corporal and a villager.

Before this happened, barely any Malaysian had heard of Sauk and the neighbouring Kampung Jenalik, which was close to the site of the siege. A site on Bukit Jenalik, in the jungle behind a primary school in the village was the base of the group.

However, hordes of journalists were being assigned to the area, and most reporters I knew wanted to be sent. All of Malaysia wanted to know what was happening in Sauk, and rushed for the papers daily for the latest word.

I don't wish to take away from the consequential terror and torture those forcibly taken underwent, nor the grief and sorrow their families must feel until today, but getting sent to Sauk was probably one of the most highly coveted assignments a news journalist could get.

But Claudia and I were a few rungs down the seniority and relevance list on the news desk at that time, with me being several years her junior. As the story grew bigger, more and more reporters were being assigned, first to Gerik, Perak where the heist occurred on 2 July, and then to Sauk. First the most senior crime desk men, then the news desk men, until, eventually, the editors needed more.

No other women higher up wanted to go, and the next obvious choices were us. The two feisty 'girls'. Intense hesitance ensued.

By the end of 4 July, I, buoyed by Claudia's determination and tenacity, put my name in the ring. Together we began our campaign to win the assignment. 'Why can't we go?'

Well, they told us the job required reporters to be camped out through the night by the side of the main street from where a dirt road led to the durian orchard where the militants were. There were no hotels in town, the closest one being in Kuala Kangsar and close to an hour away at that time on a potholed road.

There were no public toilets since everybody there actually lives there. We could be hiding in and crawling through bushes in case the commando allowed us to get a closer look of the siege area.

There would certainly be some frantic running and car chasing after army trucks and police jeeps up and down that dusty track.

One that we certainly didn't buy was that there would be leery looks from insulated townsfolk who rarely see outsiders, much less vocal and physically active 'city girls'.

Oh, and absolutely no cooperation, it seems, would come from commandos and other military officials, them being exclusively male.

'They' threw everything at us. Not all, I must add, as some rooted for us. They who knew we'd deliver the necessary coverage and wouldn't be bothered by tough situations. We sparred for almost twenty-four hours, while the 'boys' in the field were hoping for reinforcements so they could catch a nap at least occasionally.

Eventually, after even the exhausting bowel movements issue was settled, we were green-lighted. Claudia and I didn't hurrah to this openly, though, but headed downstairs to a corner behind the building to high-five and fist-punch the air with excited, and anxious, joy. The desk insisted on booking a room at the then Kuala Kangsar Rest House so us 'girls' didn't have to sleep 'rough' on site. The boys could also head there to shower and catch naps, they added. It was already four days since the heist.

We were to leave the next morning, 6 July. Claudia and I, reeling from the sudden victory of winning the assignment, sped off our respective homes, frantically threw a day bag together, and quickly texted each other to agree that we would take my little maroon Proton Tiara. I couldn't sleep that night, my body was buzzing with excitement, anxiety, pride, fear. Off we went around sunrise the next day, with a junior, male reporter in tow. He would take care of us, they told us, as we secretly rolled our eyeballs at each other. We stopped along the way to buy some large mineral water bottles. You know, just in case we needed to pee . . .

The drive to Sauk took nearly three hours, on the PLUS North-South highway, with an exit to Kuala Kangsar. We didn't even stop to throw our bags and check in at the 'rest house' in 'KK'. We were too eager to get to the epicentre.

Sauk was a forty-five-minute drive through bucolic countryside (back then, at least), on a gently winding trunk road. We nearly drove past it, because it was literally a one-street hamlet with a large open-air eatery on one side, and a row of dilapidated shops on the other.

When we got there, I saw that one of the shops had been turned into a 'media centre' of sorts by the journos who were already there, and was the first-place reinforcements like us headed to, to meet up with colleagues, get the latest updates from any official-looking person hanging about, and fresh, uncorroborated leads and gossip that would need to be confirmed later.

Heads turned as we stepped out of my car, about mid-morning. We seemed to be the only female outsiders, it seemed. As we slung our bags on, pulled out our notebooks and pens and walked toward the press centre, I heard one of the other reporters say 'Who sent them?'.

We spotted one of our editors, and went to him immediately. Looking as bored as we were keen, he said there wasn't much to do at the moment but wait. We were itching to cover something though, and I didn't want to feel useless (after all, we fought so hard to get sent) so we walked around taking notes, collecting descriptive points about the town. We spoke to some locals about how they felt about all the goings on. They seemed interested, a tad worried, but also slightly irritated. They had work to do, they needed to get on with the daily chores of everyday life in a small trading town at the centre of several agricultural villages.

Nothing much was happening. I felt a sort of pent-up tension because I was ready to roll but there was nowhere, nothing of significance to do. Several of the reporters who arrived days earlier were hanging out at the eatery, one or two walked in and out of the 'press centre' after using the toilet, and others hung about smoking. The rest of the forward team were in Jenalik Village, less than ten minutes away, close to the road to the dusun on Jenalik Hill, the base of the terrorist group's activities. They were the only outsiders allowed to go past a police roadblock just past Sauk village, and get close to the centre of the action. I was beginning to feel listless.

By this time, information was out on who exactly the insurgents were. The group was called Al-Maunah, and it began as a club for enthusiasts of a Malay self-defence art called silat, but had somehow turned rogue. Numbering twenty-nine men, they were led by a charismatic former army private called Mohamed Amin Mohamed Razali. Its demand? That then prime minister Dr Mahathir Mohamad resign, or Malaysia would face the consequences.

And so it was, for several hours, as in a classic western. The occasional rattling pick-up lorry driving past, blowing up clouds of dust, flies buzzing over small plates of kueh on the tables at the one restaurant, locals chatting excitedly about the comings and goings of army, police and media vehicles, residents driving into and out of town from the kampung nearby, and reporters walking around looking for any detail they could use in a story.

Occasionally, one of our colleagues would come into town from the *kampung* aka the 'front line' outside the army and police cordon, and feed us with as much information as they'd managed to gather from security forces, and we'd help by writing up a story using those facts, and calling it in, through the public phone, to the editors back in KL.

Most of that day passed like this, for us in Sauk, at least. A lot of things had gone on in the jungle in the past few days, much of which has been written about post-incident (there's even a History Channel documentary on what came to be called the Sauk Siege).

These included commandos infiltrating the group's camp, a significant amount of gunfire aimed at keeping the militants awake through the night, and much psychological warfare, according to the powers that be on the scene. However, all of it was confined to the actual dusun and immediate surroundings.

Then, late in the day, we heard police sirens. As the sound got closer, all the locals and reporters in town walked out to the dusty curb of the main road. Police lorries and vans whizzed by. They were full of men, some shirtless, with their arms behind their backs. The siege was over. The 'terrorists' were captured. The Sauk Siege was over.

For Claudia and I, it felt like the incident was over almost as soon as it had begun, at least for us. In that moment, it felt like we never really got to be part of the 'action' closer to the front line, so to speak, where the reporters who went earlier were. But for all of those directly involved, it was the end of a five-day nightmare. For some, the consequences would last longer.

Claudia and I were devastated to hear later about the two hostages who were killed in the incident, Army Corporal Matthew anak Medan and Police Detective Corporal Raju Saghadevan. The other two hostages, Police Sergeant Mohd Shah Ahmad and villager Jaafar Puteh were rescued by the forces.

Claudia and I soon realized, though, that although the whole drama was over, our work was not done. We finally had a chance to work on some meatier stories, after being assigned to the 'easier' colour pieces in town. Although the terrorists were removed from the scene, the authorities were still about. I saw that most of the reporters were driving off chasing the police lorries to wherever they were headed to process the perpetrators. The rest of us remained, gaping through the dust they left behind. The rest of us hoped to gain access to the dusun.

While hoping, we got busy. We tried to interview some of the police and army personnel involved in the capture and rescue operations.

Never once did we face the cold shoulder spoken of earlier. Claudia and I were treated like just one of the reporters. There was no partiality to the men. There were none of the once-overs. We felt . . . included. Questions were asked, conversations flowed, notes were scribbled, stories were filed. Night came and, exhausted more from the excitement than the exertion, we turned to my little car, and drove to our faded rest house in Kuala Kangsar with strict instructions from our editor on the ground to head back to Sauk first thing in the morning.

And the real coup, for me personally, did really come the next day. My editor had been able to arrange for two of us to enter the dusun. After some negotiations, he managed to persuade the authorities to allow two from his team to enter. Not many others wanted to. Post-siege, the big story was where the captured men were, so most had left town with the terrorists. My editor had three of us 'leftovers' to pick from, and he chose Claudia and me. She the more senior, and between me and the other guy, I was the writer, and he the reporter.

We all know how some journalists are reporters and others are writers. This job required a writer. Someone who could describe the place where thirty men camped for five days with a huge number of stolen arms and ammunition, plotted plans to take over Kuala Lumpur, and tortured and killed hostages in vivid detail. I was nervous about what I would find. I imagined a battlefield scene, blood all over the ground, weaponry strewn everywhere and, from sheer overdramatization, grey clouds with an approaching storm in the sky.

And so, I went with Claudia. We were finally in! We hitched a ride with a local policeman because my little hatchback would not be able to make it up the dirt track. As soon as I got in the car, and it started moving, I put all my senses to work, and began taking notes, way before we even got to Kampung Jenalik, the primary school and the foothill of Bukit Jenalik.

Everything I had been taught in the first years of my career as a journalist came back, but they began clashing with all the thoughts I had now about what I needed to do. 'Just take key points down', 'focus on your end story and search for information that will fit there', and so on were some of the things I was told to do to be a quicker reporter on the beat covering ministers and businessmen, but this time I had no end goal, no conclusive narrative in mind. I had to keep it as open as possible, we had no idea what we were going to find. Write EVERYTHING down, Seema! I told myself. Feel everything, smell it, breathe it, listen.

And so I did. When we finally got there, I filled my notebook with the sights, smells and sounds of the place. I even absorbed the crunch of the ground under my sneakers as I walked from tree to tree and eventually halfway down to the brook crossing the site.

For a place that saw bloodshed, it was calm. The hair at the back of my neck cooled as I felt a light breeze. I couldn't hear the road or airplanes or machinery. I could hear the rustle of the leaves on the ground around me and from the durian trees. I smelled blood, that metallic scent. The smell of death. I saw what I thought was a piece of flesh on the ground, and some blood stains.

There wasn't a buzz of activity, considering it was a place which, half a day ago saw the biggest terrorist attack in Malaysia. Only some soldiers and policemen walking about looking at trenches and freshly dug graves.

It looked like a peaceful grove, and I remember thinking that it would make the perfect picnic spot, or a hiker's campsite. I would have wanted to picnic or camp here. Except for the smell of durian in the air, which came next after the scent of blood. I hate durian.

We had to leave. We were allowed no more than half an hour there. We didn't want to go, not so soon, because there was so much more to explore. But the policeman rushed us, and hustled us back to his car.

That exploration was the exciting part of the job. It's always fun (though it's distasteful to use that word for this incident), to be on the scene, asking questions, looking at things, watching them happen, writing it all down. But when you get back, you have to write it all down into a story. We didn't have a laptop. No handphone to type into. We had our notebooks. My editor, brusque as usual, wanted the story sent, then and there, to the editors back in KL before we left for home.

He wanted a feature story from me, not a quick, short report. But a descriptive feature on the campsite with all the atmospheric details. I took my notebook full of excited scribbles to that open-air restaurant by the main road, and sat in a quiet corner. I ordered an iced coffee, and started flipping pages.

Back and forth I went. Where do I begin? Two hours, three iced coffees and a noteful of scribblings later I managed to squeeze out a story, my pen running dry. I'm the sort of writer that this quote by George R.R. Martin is perfect for: 'Some writers enjoy writing, I am told. Not me. I enjoy having written.'

I felt an immense sense of relief as I crossed the road to where my editor was standing beside the phone booth. I passed him the notebook. As he flipped through it, I thought to myself 'Please don't send me back to rewrite it. He's the toughest editor I've ever had. Was I too flower-y? Too feminine? Too wordy, not descriptive enough?' He looked up a few minutes later and said 'Ok, call the desk' pointing to the phone in the booth.

And that's how I sent in my article, by reading it slowly and carefully over the phone, mouthing every comma and apostrophe, to a writer typing it into the PC on the other end. That experience taught me to 'swallow the frog' as the saying goes. Sometimes, you've just got to knuckle down and do the hard thing then and then, and it is a skill I gained then. To be able to put everything else in life aside, against a running clock, focus the attention on one thing, and produce. Produce it well.

Besides relief at finishing the job, I experienced another sensation. A feeling of satisfaction. I was able to contribute something, albeit something very small, to this story in Malaysia's history, after all. After being thrown all the reasons we couldn't cover this, and having our assignment cut short (thankfully) due to the quick actions of the authorities to capture the insurgents, I was still able to provide a proper piece of coverage on one of the country's biggest terror attacks, giving Malaysia some idea of the 'scene of the crime' so to speak.

That's all I ask, really. To be given an opportunity to tell a story. And this is something that took with me throughout my career. The conviction to ask, argue, debate, demand in some cases, for my seat at the table. It taught me gumption. Or was that something I already had? Even if I did, that incident served me more. Claudia's strong sense of gumption fed my own, and somehow, we snatched this part of Malaysian history and put our names on a very long list of the people it affected.

Soon after the stories were filed through that beat up and much-used phone booth clad in faded blue and orange, we prepared to head to KL. We'd already cleared out our room at the Kuala Kangsar rest house that morning, so all we had to do was pile back into my car and drive back down that single lane trunk road toward home.

But we decided to take a detour. Or rather, journey further up Route 76 for an hour or so to check out the scenery, road-side fruit stalls, and Chenderoh Lake along the way. The drive paid off, the views were serene and idyllic.

We stopped beside the marshy Chenderoh Lake, a man-made body of water built in the twenties as a hydroelectric dam, several hamlets, and many rambutan and durian stalls where locals sold fruit harvested from their own family orchards.

Despite my many protests, my passengers managed to convince me to allow them to pack my cat boot with durian.

That was when I was left with one of the memories of this whole adventure I will never forget. You see, we'd just come off the terrorists' campsite, didn't change clothes, didn't shower. We had that smell of death stuck to us. Combine that with the heady aroma of *durian kampung* or village durian, and you have this thick, pungent odour that made me gag. We drove home with it, but even with our windows down, it wouldn't leave. My car smelled of that for a week after we returned, even though I had it washed and vacuumed a couple of times. And I can still recall that scent today. It's what I think of every time I pass a durian stall. That stench literally fills my nostrils every time someone mentions eating durian. It's probably why I hate the fruit so much.

Death and durians aside, something Claudia, one of those intrepid reporters many in our industry looked up to, said stuck with me. She said now we can cover other, bigger things. Things like this! And people can't say 'no', because they know we'd done it. They'll have to give us the assignment.

More importantly, I thought, it meant that having fought for the opportunity to do bigger, more challenging stories, and actually doing it didn't just mean something to others, but also to me.

Afterword: In the weeks, months and years to come, the insurgents would be charged with 'waging war against the King' of Malaysia, undergo a lengthy trial process, and eventually be sentenced to, depending on where each stood in Al-Maunah's ranks, life imprisonment, ten years in jail or death by hanging as was the case for Amin and his three lieutenants. 2020 is the twentieth anniversary of that event, and some of the rebels are out of prison now.

*Claudia Theophilus passed away in 2013 while on holiday with friends in Lebanon, aged forty-two.

My Hong Kong Journey: From Handover to Protests and Pandemic

By Jervina Lao

1 July 1997.

The date was etched in history. The return of Hong Kong by the United Kingdom to China. For journalists, it was one of those events that made a résumé stand out. I knew I had to be in Hong Kong to cover the handover ceremony. It was the place to be and that was where I was going to be, regardless of who or what I had to screw over to get there.

In April 1997, I quit my job as a senior reporter of an international news agency where I worked for two years and joined *Agence France Presse* (AFP) in Hong Kong. The French news agency had an international English news service with an Asian headquarter that was and still is in Hong Kong. My role was as correspondent/editor. I had wondered aloud what that meant as the two roles were often adversarial. A colleague had smiled and said, 'It means you're not just a writer. You edit as well.' Translation: I didn't just get to have my stories mangled, I got to return the favour.

I was no stranger to Hong Kong. I had visited the city when I was a child with my parents in the late seventies. My memory of Hong Kong then was of a crowded, stinky, and noisy city. Immigration officials were abrupt and rude, swearing at every Chinese face that didn't speak Cantonese.

Yet when I arrived in Hong Kong in May 1997, I was no longer the impressionable child clinging to her parents, agog at a strange city.

I was an excited journalist conscious of snagging a front seat to history. I was also conscious of being female and Asian. It was a rare combination in the white male world of the international news industry. In the AFP headquarters, I was the only Asian female correspondent. I knew getting the job was a major coup. Each day, I showed up early and had to be chased out of the office to go home. I loved my work but there was no respite from the effort to ensure that I brought my A-game every single day. It was exhausting. My competitive personality likely didn't help. I was born in a family with a surplus of boys hence I grew up learning early to assert myself. Every day that I walked into the office my stomach would churn with the fear that my best might not be enough.

I enjoyed living in Hong Kong in 1997. It was different from Manila and the other cities I visited and worked in. There was a vibe to Hong Kong, an energy that was unique to the city. People walked fast, talked fast and worked fast. Things happened at warp speed. Hong Kong was the ultimate party paradise. Rave parties began at 8 a.m. and lasted till the next day. Scantily dressed, mascara smeared women would stumble out into the street from bars at 7 a.m., the time I would return home after completing an overnight shift at the newsroom.

Yet the city, famed for being a swashbuckling uber-capitalist outpost of democracy was to be to be handed over to the staid control-freak communist China. Were the Hong Kongers worried about Beijing crimping their style? Hong Kongers prided themselves for being practical. Those who were pessimistic had already sold up and left for Singapore, Canada, Australia, UK, and the United States years and months earlier.

One of my close Chinese-Filipino friends who lived in Hong Kong for years and whose father gifted her with an apartment near tourists' shopping mecca Causeway Bay, left the city and moved to Canada. 'I don't trust the communists,' she said, not surprising for the daughter of immigrants who fled to the Philippines from China to escape Mao Zedong's Red Army. Nevertheless, she kept her multi-million-dollar apartment and rented it out for enough money to fund her new life in a democratic Western country.

The Hong Kongers who remained fell into two categories. The first were those who were wary but reassured by the Basic Law and Beijing's 'one-country, two systems' policy that allowed Hong Kong to keep its liberties, systems and way of life for fifty years. The second were those who were gung-ho about the 'return to the motherland'.

In 1997, China was just renewing its economic relationships with the West after its communist government slammed shut the country's gates following the 1989 Tiananmen Square crackdown and the consequent Western sanctions. Hong Kong saw itself as the West's bridge to understanding China and Beijing's bridge to understanding the West. More so, Hong Kongers believed they would transform China. Make it more democratic. Hong Kong's handover would be the classic corporate reverse takeover. Or so Hong Kongers thought.

In most of my man-on-the-street interviews in the run-up to the handover, very few Hong Kongers expressed concern over the future of the city. Many said they trusted the UK to ensure that China complied with the Basic Law. Besides, 'it wouldn't make any sense for China to kill the golden goose'. Hong Kong was the envy of many cities in Asia. China wouldn't do anything to damage this status, would they?

What did my British colleagues in the newsroom feel?

I was one of two Asians in an editorial desk staffed by mostly Westerners. I was Filipino, my other Asian colleague was Indian. Neither of us felt any nostalgia for the British empire. The same, however, was not true for our British colleagues. On the evening of 1 July 1997, bottles of wine were opened and drunk—not in celebration of a new era but in sorrow over the end of one. The handover was not a surprise. Then British prime minister Margaret Thatcher agreed in 1985 to return sovereignty of Hong Kong to China. However, for many Brits, it marked the end of the British Empire. I recalled witnessing a few of my hard-nosed colleagues surreptitiously wipe a tear when Prince Charles and Hong Kong's last British governor Chris Patten boarded the HMY Britannia and sailed away.

A few days after the handover, on 4 July, one of my still desolate British colleagues asked an American colleague what US holiday it was, 'Thanksgiving Day, innit?' To which the American snapped, 'Nope. It's Independence Day.'

Fast forward to twenty plus years later. In January 2019, I came full circle returning to Hong Kong with a husband and two teenagers.

My family and I had moved to Hong Kong after nearly twenty years in Singapore because my husband had taken up a new job in the city.

I had left AFP and Hong Kong in 1999, returned home to Manila to take a breather before moving to Singapore to join the local newspaper. A male ex-colleague congratulated me for leaving the gruelling world of wire news agencies, saying 'Good on you. You escaped becoming a misfit like the other women.' I remember being appalled by the misogyny behind those words. 'Why do you say that?' I asked. 'Kate Webb still works and she's fantastic!' He shuffled uncomfortably before saying, 'Well, she's never married or had kids. A misfit.'

Kate Webb was an Australian war correspondent renowned for being captured and held prisoner by the North Vietnamese during the Vietnam War. She was a legend among her peers. A year after her death in 2007, a prize was set up by AFP in her name for Asian journalists who have braved dangerous conditions while working in Asia.

I for one felt honoured to have worked with her briefly when she was parachuted in from Jakarta where she was bureau chief to help with the coverage of the Hong Kong handover. To hear her called a 'misfit' because she hadn't married or reproduced had summarized for me all the prejudice that women faced to get ahead in journalism.

Therefore, it was with delight tinged with a dash of envy that I met Asian women holding senior positions in major Western newspapers when I attended an event hosted by the Asian American Journalist Association in Hong Kong in 2019. Women like Kate Webb paved the way for journalists like me and them.

And yet for every woman who climbed the ladder of success in industry, there are many more women like me who have decided to pull back their career and focus on their family. Did I marry and bear children because I didn't want to be labelled a 'misfit'? Was I a sell-out?

The first time I came across the protesters was on a Sunday in May 2019. My family had just had lunch in a restaurant in Wanchai. We were making our way home when hundreds of placard-carrying people chanting slogans clogged the streets.

'What's going on, Mama?' my sons asked me. It was the first time ever that they had seen a protest as such marches were unheard of in

Singapore. This protest was still peaceful but it was just the start of many more that became progressively violent.

The protesters said they were fighting against Beijing's attempt to erode their rights. Yet for many Asian journalists, the protests were incomprehensible.

Former Singaporean news colleagues agreed with their Prime Minister Lee Hsien Loong who said in an interview that the protesters' demands 'are not demands which are meant to be a programme to solve Hong Kong's problems. Those are demands which are intended to humiliate and bring down the government.'

How can they complain about police violence, scoffed some of my former Filipino colleagues on social media? Was there a shoot to kill order like the one Philippine President Rodrigo Duterte handed to Manila cops when confronting suspected drug dealers? After months of protests and riots, there were still no official deaths unlike in Jakarta where five people died and more than 250 were injured in a month of student protests and violence.

Many foreign residents sympathized with the protest cause but deplored the turbulence. 'This violence just has to stop,' a long-time American resident in Hong Kong told me in one the various forums that had sprouted to talk about the protests.

One thing was certain though, Hong Kongers were frightened but defiant. Some of the young people who I had met and had spoken with said they felt driven to march despite knowing their actions were futile.

'If nothing happens, then I go to Taiwan,' a young female protester said.

The parties stopped. Famous party central, Lan Kwai Fong, was just a block from where the protesters and police battled it out with tear gas and petrol bombs surrounded by skyscrapers housing global financial institutions and luxury shopping brands like Hermes and Cartier. The international acts such as opera tenor Jose Carreras cancelled. Daily Show host and comedian Trevor Noah skipped Hong Kong for Singapore. Suddenly, Hong Kong was the happening place but for the wrong happenings.

As a journalist, it was the perfect time and place to work. Once again, I was in the middle of history being made, albeit this time inadvertently.

Approaching various news outlets should be a no-brainer to any working journalist. But as a wife whose husband was employed in an industry that suffered greatly from the protests and as a mother worried that her teenage sons might find themselves in trouble with the government should they be drawn to the demonstrations out of curiosity, the calculation to return to the news industry was no longer simple. As a journalist, I sympathized with the protesters who were desperate to protect their freedoms. But as a wife and mother, I found myself in communion with the other side. The side that wanted peace and prosperity at all costs. The side that was a sell-out.

Hong Kong protesters said they wanted China to observe the Basic Law till 2047 and beyond. Therefore, they believed anything the government of the Hong Kong Special Administrative Region did, would undermine the Basic Law. As far as the protesters were concerned, everything and anything from the government that favoured Beijing should meet with a big fat N-O. What happened to Hong Kong's famous practicality? It appeared to have disappeared leaving only desperation.

The Hong Kongers' relationship with Beijing and their fear of losing their liberties brought to mind my son's pet worm when he was at primary school. His teacher had told the class not to overfeed the worm. He was so scared of harming the animal that he refused to do anything or let anything be done for it. He didn't feed it, didn't give it water, didn't put any soil. Just left it in the plastic cup hoping that it would stay the same way when it was first given to him. In the end, the worm died and ended up in the trash to copious tears and gnashing of teeth.

The violence and the protests went on a hiatus during Christmas 2019 but it was the pandemic that snuffed it out. The last protest concerned the National Security Law that Beijing enacted for Hong Kong but that died quickly. Is this the end of the Fragrant Harbour? The double whammy of protests and pandemic has dented the city's economy and threw Hong Kongers off their stride.

At the time of this writing, the coronavirus pandemic has ravaged the world for more than eighteen months. Under the National Security Law, opposition politicians were detained and dissenting voices silenced. Many foreign and local families have upped stakes and left the city.

Has Hong Kong lost its mojo?

Commentators mourned that Hong Kong was becoming a normal Chinese city. But what was a normal Chinese city? A place like Shanghai, Guangzhou or Beijing—vibrant, modern, wealthy? Or cities where money was king and residents thrived only if they kept their heads down and their mouths shut?

The Greek philosopher Heraclitus said the only thing constant in life is change. I know I have changed. Motherhood has changed me. I, the fearless reporter, who once faced the gun of a rebel soldier without flinching have found myself a wretched wreck each time my sons stayed out late during the height of the protests. There were many nights that I wondered whether I have lost my mojo.

As for Hong Kong, the inevitability of change was written into the Basic Law. The rights promised to the city was to end in 2047. Would this be a disaster or a relief? No one yet knows. The only consolation I and Hong Kongers can likely get is from French writer Jean-Baptiste Alphonse Karr who in 1849 wrote: '*Plus ça change, plus c'est la meme chose.*' The more things change, the more they stay the same.

Journeys of a Lifetime

By Amandra M. Megarani

I was only eight years old when our family took a 7,700 km round trip across three great islands of Indonesia, from the top corner of Sumatra going south, then the length of Java, and continuing on to Bali. Instead of taking a short flight or an inter-island bus, our 1991 white Honda Civic hatchback carried us through the sharply curved roads of Barisan Mountains, winding along between breathtaking river valleys and steep cliffs. My Dad, with his great sense of adventure, sat placidly in the driver's seat while me and my four-year-old sister plopped in the back. As we came across the famous 'Kelok 44'—an impressive mountain side passage of forty-four curves in Agam county—I remember Mom's anxiety each time we made a hairpin turn. But all that heart-stopping action certainly paid off as we reached the peak, gazing at the expanse of Maninjau Lake, 461.5 m above sea level.

Sometimes I switched seats with my mother so she could tend to my carsick sister. Mesmerized by the scenery, I took it all in. Each changing landscape brought with it a particular rhythm, a variety of smells, a different accent, sometimes local languages that I didn't understand. We passed through shadowy areas that are supposed to be forbidden at night or other places considered haunted or mystical, but I looked on with fascination without any fear.

Despite the heat and being nestled in a little car among a month's worth of luggage, I still feel a great sense of wonder when I remember that trip. Having spent so much time reading books and perusing National Geographic magazines and letting my mind wander to all the places and events in their stories made the experience of the journey itself really come alive. Even as a child, noting the facts and figures of places and events happening was second nature to me. Faithfully, I held a map in hand and traced the route we travelled, noting each city we passed and eagerly awaiting the next.

That long-lasting thirst for new experience and adventure eventually led my path to become a journalist, although little did I know back then what the full scope of the profession entailed. After securing a job with Tempo, one of the most trusted magazines in Indonesia, I began as a reporter for News and Economy desk. Like most new recruits, I was trained to cover daily news under deadline pressure, mostly working in the office or attending seminars around the city, hardly what you would call adventurous. The coveted special reports are usually assigned to more seasoned reporters, but I was young, living in the capital city independently for the first time, eager to learn and happily living for my job.

I was lucky. Two months after being accepted working full-time, I was given an assignment to stand in for a senior writer that was unable to make a trip to Makassar for a special coverage on economic growth in Eastern Indonesia. Given unprecedented freedom to plan my itinerary and schedule, I was quite surprised and a bit nervous—but that feeling was quickly pushed aside by the delight I felt from a dream come true. This was what I have been waiting for.

Supplied with only two contact persons and a two-way plane ticket, I made my way there. Greeted by a largely seafaring community, clear blue skies free from pollution, old colonial fortresses and beautiful ports lined with traditional fishing boats with their distinct *phinisi* sails, I can feel the thrill of adventure rushing back. I visited national parks filled with butterflies in Bantimurung and passed through prehistoric caves with the oldest signs of human drawings in Indonesia. But the most memorable moment was the sight of a herd of horses galloping freely in a field of tall grass, set against dark, towering karst cliffs right outside my car window in the region of Maros. Memories of my childhood washed over me, as I remember feeling awed by the striking images of lakes and valleys that we passed throughout our journey. I knew that this is the life I wanted.

Doubts about my job began to fade as I found my way around the region, listening to the friendly locals as they tell stories of their lives, happy with the economic growth of their city, and even some women began to hold the role of breadwinners (carrier woman) of the family. As part of a large family myself (being the oldest of five sisters) I also wanted to have this experience. I came back feeling validated and brimming with information, convinced that I have chosen the right career.

Five months later, I got married. Despite the skepticism of my co-workers, I still believed I could handle the job. Of course I realized that the challenges ahead won't be easy. The employee turnover in the media business is high, and they predicted that I wouldn't last more than another year. Many women couldn't keep juggling time between the demands of being a journalist, being married, and the responsibilities of having children.

But I wasn't deterred. My mom herself was a dedicated career woman as she raised five children with my dad. Being a journalist, doing reports and travelling is my childhood dream, but raising a family is also a phase of life that I want to have. I was determined that I could balance my time and responsibilities and do it well.

Nevertheless, I am no magician. It would be very inconvenient for me to travel far, so I was moved to the city desk. I practically worked exclusively with city issues for the next three years. I spent all my energy in getting married, being pregnant, giving birth, nursing my baby exclusively and still keeping up with work as a news reporter. But one of the perks of being a journalist is having some flexibility in office hours. Taking turns with my husband to leave the house, and with the help of family members and child care services, I can still keep it together— still tired to the bone though! I also had to push aside guilty feelings as I left my son to work, but felt joy in being involved with my son's development.

Even as my scope of work was defined within the city, I still discovered a sense of adventure. No matter where I go, I always find something new in Jakarta. It is a densely populated melting pot, home to glamorous skyscrapers and hidden slums, entangled between never-ending bureaucracy and convoluted dealings of slippery businessmen. It is endlessly fascinating, a different kind of adventure that I can access while still being connected to my family.

As my firstborn son reached his second year, I was given an assignment abroad, still related to my job in the city. I was to travel to Singapore and report on its Mass Rapid Transport system as Jakarta was developing its own to solve its ever-saturating traffic congestion. This was not my first trip there, but it was still a pleasure to see the changes it went through. My three-day trip felt like a breath of fresh air, a little break, after struggling so long. Not only that, it also helped me achieve my personal plan to wean my firstborn.

After that, things got better. I was promoted, moved back to economy desk and received more travel assignments—Banda Aceh, Medan, Bandung, Denpasar, even as far as Kuala Lumpur and Tokyo. I even had the opportunity to take one-and-a-half years of paid leave to continue my studies. After completing my Master's degree in Communication, I chatted with the senior co-worker who predicted that I would only last a year. 'I was definitely mistaken. I really thought you wouldn't last,' he admitted to me.

In 2015, I started writing features for Art and Culture, the middle-pages/intermezzo sections of the *Tempo* weekly magazine. This theme was more aligned with my interests and bachelor degree background in Interior Design, and I thoroughly enjoyed writing about art galleries, dance productions, history, culture, architecture and stories of prominent public figures.

Two years later, I landed a huge travel assignment, a report on the 350-year anniversary of the Treaty of Breda (31 July 1667), a treaty that ended the Second Anglo-Dutch War between England, the Dutch Republic, France, and Denmark-Norway. The treaty resulted in the transfer of Run, a nutmeg-producing island in the Banda archipelago—which was under English rule—in exchange for an island now known as Manhattan, which was previously held by the Dutch. Yes, that Manhattan, now part of New York City and the eleventh biggest agglomeration in the world. In contrast, I have never heard of Run, and struggled to find it even as some maps failed to mention it at all—although to be fair there are 17,491 islands in this country and a few more being discovered once in a while.

Such was the isolation of this island that to reach it, first you needed to fly to Ambon, then ride a ferry to Banda Naira, which is only available once in every three-four days. From there, you must find a locally sourced motorboat that only leaves once in the morning and once in the evening to the island. Often it cannot cross when the weather is rough and waves reach five-seven metres.

What a journey that would be! It would take at least seven-ten days of travel, if everything goes well. The mystery of the location, the rich historical element and allure of this trip is incredibly tantalizing. But also, at this time I already have a second-born. He was only seven months old and he was still breastfeeding exclusively and still learning how to eat solid food. I was rocked between the possibilities of travel and the consequences of it. Would it be possible to arrange my family affairs, even go so far as to take everyone with me to make it there?

In the end, I decided it was too unpredictable and strenuous to put a remote trip together like that. I have come full circle, and it is now time for me to do what my senior once had done, and delegate the trip to another co-worker. As I did nine years ago, she would be my ears, eyes and mouth throughout this challenging assignment, gathering information in my place.

And so, as she described perilous crossings on a boat crammed with cement sacks, wood planks, and fresh produce; the extremely limited source of power, fresh water or telecommunication signals; solemn remnants of old colonial plantation buildings; and the fragrant smell of nutmeg drying under the hot sun, wafting from each house; I could only imagine myself in her shoes, absorbing what must be an exotic, harsh island so far removed from my crowded city. As a reporter I still feel the excitement from listening about these narratives, albeit second-hand. Its bloody history of colonial trade and war is shocking and yet seductive, the information-gathering my second nature. If my assignment years ago in Makassar, spoke of progress, hope, and the shifting lifestyle of a growing community, this is a story of stillness, isolation and a modest life, a place where clamorous national policies of development and modernization failed to anchor its grip.

It brings me to question my own immobility, now as a mother and a wife. I ask myself - have I just forfeited the journey of my lifetime? Have I sacrificed my passion for my motherhood roles? I would give anything for my children—yet I know that doesn't mean I'm giving up.

Not all journeys are meant to be taken, and this time I let it be traversed through someone else. But I believe it is not resigned forever, only postponed for the future. I am sure someday I will go on these great voyages with my husband and children, exploring the world, having our adventures together in good time—the way I did with my parents and sister more than twenty years ago. Because, sometimes the joy of travel is only real when shared, especially with people you love.

Travel is not just about moving from place to place, sightseeing or meeting new people. Essentially travel is about building the self, expanding the mind and growing in maturity. If I was once inspired to be a journalist to explore, write, and spread information to push for change and improvement, perhaps one day my children will do even more—be an agent of change themselves for this country, by their travel experiences.

I have always cherished my job as a reporter, grateful for the chance to visit places, learn new things and write coverages with all their challenges every day. I also treasure my role as a mother. To me, they are not a contradiction. I don't have to choose one over the other. They are complementary, both part of a whole, it's who I am.

A Name at all Costs

By Melizarani T. Selva

An airplane disappears from the sky and it is the best time for a journalist to be alive. No one admits this out loud. We embody this truth in the way our newsroom moves at 6.15 a.m. Giddy with a rare and cruel excitement. It is 8 March 2014 and Malaysia Airlines Flight MH370 is missing. This has never happened before and yet, within my radius, it feels like we have waited our entire careers for this moment to arrive. A dozen drowsy editorial staff and I tumble over ethics and each other, tunneling through people, to retrieve the story of the century.

It happened on my day off. One final Saturday before my mandatory month of field reporting training ended. Come Monday, I would assume my role as the youngest sub-editor of *New Straits Times*, my second-choice profession. No journalist roles were available at the time. I savoured every minor assignment and filler story I could write. The chance of a lifetime arrived when the office secretary rang, 'You are being recalled. Please report to the desk ASAP.'

She did not explain why but she did not have to.

Minutes before she dialled my number, my father had woken me up: 'MAS Aircraft went missing.

Go to the office now.

You should not miss this.'

For any other daughter, this kind of wake-up call would seem odd and disconcerting. For me, the daughter of a famed senior journalist in a rival newspaper, this was a tip-off. A head start in a race to scoop the superior story.

We both knew what the front page would be. A list of names. A gut-wrenching list of incomplete names and faces of the people on board, human lives that were missing. It was too early to tell the fate of the passengers, whether they would be counted as survivors or bodies. We did not know which airspace the plane was in, but we knew that the most powerful story in a mass tragedy can rest in the name of a single passenger. One full name was all we needed to reveal their next-of-kin, their motivation for being on that flight to Beijing and ultimately the human-interest story, worthy of page three.

Full names are preferred, pseudonyms are discouraged and anonymity is the last resort. In the first twelve hours, my colleagues and I exhausted all means we had to gather names of the passenger manifest. We called friends of friends we barely knew, scoured Facebook pages of ex-lovers who worked as flight crew and texted estranged cousins, in search of a source. One qualified person to break a story, any story. We were high on the fumes of second-hand grief and the prospect of a front-page by-line. Declaring our mission and presence in the same cold call courtesy that had been trained into our psyche, we began our quest for passenger names with the same script 'Hello, my name is _____ from *New Straits Times*.' Some gave us information we already had. Few spilled tears and helpful sentences. Most hung up after asking how we got their number.

I was an eager cub reporter with two days left to prove myself before a life of sub-editing stories instead of writing them. I had no names to offer and was determined to make a name for myself, or at least, shake off the nickname 'T. Selva's daughter' that followed me throughout the media industry. It wasn't a bad nickname, it was just a heavy one, commonly thrust upon 'legacy hires' like myself. If I succeed, it is assumed that my father had something to do with it. If I failed, didn't my father teach me anything? Either way, the only path towards carrying the weight of my own name is to earn a byline.

Luck and convenient misfortune led me to Tharish, a friend of the guy I had just started seeing. Tharish posted a hopeful tribute on Facebook, to her best friend's family, a rich and prominent family, who was on the doomed flight. I zeroed in on this opportunity of turning her into a source. She could be my story. All Tharish had to do was give me the name of her best friend. And maybe a bit of their last conversation? And maybe her raw reaction towards the unprecedented news about a missing plane? And maybe just a bit more details for a follow up human interest piece?

My mind envisioned a dozen possible headlines.

In an ideal world of journalism practice, the kind a Mass Comm degree prepares us for, I would first need to engage Tharish as a journalist's source, with immense care and patience. As much as I recognized her existence as valuable intel, she needed to agree to be part of this one-way information transaction. Upon her yes or no, only then could I proceed to interview her. But we were not in my college classroom. Nothing about our situation was ideal. Didn't Tharish realize that she was a valuable source? A breaking news goldmine! I saw nothing but the next story. With ruthless courtesy and no prior interaction, I loaded our Messenger chat window with questions about her best friend's name, family and home address. Tharish offered scant bits of information and then stopped replying. I prodded her for a response.

Nothing.

Before I could convey my impatience to the grieving woman, my editor Sharanjit summons me to his desk, saving me from burning the bridge of our fragile acquaintanceship. Sharanjit is the designated editor in charge of the day and he sits on an elevated platform in the middle of the newsroom, surrounded by a dozen television screens blaring BREAKING NEWS. He is on the phone while two other phones continue to ring and I can't tell if he is enjoying this. It is 2.45 p.m. and we are running out of time to fill tomorrow's newspaper. Every fact we know lapses in validity within hours. Sources rapidly grow stale. The plane remains lost and here we are trying to report a tragedy that has not yet taken place.

Sharanjit jots down an address on a torn piece of paper and hangs up the phone after three pleasant Thank yous. He hands me the address of Sergeant Hamid Roslan, the father of MH370 passenger Norli Akmar. 'Get the family's reaction to the news. Send in the story by 4 p.m.' I accepted my deployment without asking him the question on my mind 'How? How do I ask a father what he feels about his daughter being lost in the sky?' I drive my mother's Hyundai Atos above its preferred speed limit. It trembles and threatens to break down as I try to find the right words to form the most painfully redundant interview question: 'How do you feel right now?'

When I arrive, a swarm of TV News anchors and their vans have crowded the entrance of the police residential quarters. I am too late and have no idea what my interviewee looks like. There is a commotion brewing between the press and neighbours. Someone's parked car is blocking another car. Something about the media invading their privacy. There is no way in. My phone rings and it is my father calling to ask 'So, what story are you writing?' I fight the urge to tell him everything. Today, he is not my father. He is my competition. I hang up and devise a plan to break into the police quarters.

I sneak away from the entrance, searching for a side gate of some sort and locate a low wall about eight feet tall. It is precisely at this moment that I realize that I am dressed for a desk job and a date from the night before. A colourful ankle-length dress with no time for regrets. I tied the ends of my fabric to fashion a lungi and conjured the upper body strength of coconut tree climbers I had seen in Tamil movies, to scale the wall and hoist myself onto the other side. My feet land inside the compound with a neat thud and not a single bruise. I was thrilled. Guided by adrenaline and eavesdropping, I located the family's unit on the second floor but when I reached the final flight of stairs, I found an army of reporters furiously typing out quotes from a man who was no longer there.

'*Dia baru je keluar! Dah nak pergi KLIA!*'[1] a Berita Harian reporter said to me.

The father had just left to join the other next-of-kin at KLIA airport. I missed him by a minute.

'*Itu! Itu dia kat sana! Belum masuk kereta lagi!*'[2] the reporter called out as I ran down the stairs to catch him for a comment, before he entered the car. His kindly neighbours had wisened up and began

---

[1]Translation: 'He just left! He is about to go to KLIA (Kuala Lumpur International Airport)'.

[2]Translation: 'There! There he is! He hasn't entered the car yet!'

ushering him away from the media. I was so close and right there, but they had not seen me yet.

I recalled the crude synonym for the word 'journalist'—'ambulance chasers'. At one of the many breakfasts I've had with my father, he told me a story of how he tossed his media badge, roughed up his office attire and became a volunteer to help carry victims of the Highland Towers collapse, into an ambulance. No one was ready to talk about their feelings to a well-dressed journalist with a deadline. They're in shock and they need comfort, said my father. Care, that only another human being can provide. When my father recounts this story, he cements it with two lessons:

We go where the story goes.

We do whatever it takes.

Footsteps away from Sergeant Hamid Roslan, I borrow my father's thirty-three years of journalistic experience and perform what it means to be a person. I pull off my media lanyard and reach into my handbag for a packet of tissues. His face is grimaced with sweat and tears he is unable to hold. I reach my arm through the mob of well-meaning neighbours to offer him a tissue. He pulls one out and turns to face me. For a brief second, I abandon the English language and negotiate my position to reach his side. I ask him if he needs another tissue and if he has heard from his daughter, in the same breath. His mouth spills repeated truths. *Anak saya. My child.*

Anak saya. My child.

Holiday. She needed a break. Miscarriage.

My child lost her child.

Norli Akmar Hamid, thirty-three years old, boarded flight MH370 with her husband, Mohd Razahan Zamani. It was supposed to be a holiday, delayed honeymoon and her first time on a plane. The couple had recently suffered a miscarriage and this trip was to help them heal.

I had my story.

Upon revealing the tragedy within the tragedy, Sergeant Hamid stops talking. He realizes that I am not just any person with a tissue packet. He is unaware that I have a voice recorder in the shallow pocket of my dress, but he senses that my attention towards him is different from the rest. He asks me sharply 'Where are you from?' I tell him that I am from NST and recite my scripted protocol to legally quote him for my story. He nods grimly and briskly brushes past me to reach his car door. The kindly neighbours grow more protective and physical towards all story hunters. 'Media *tepi*! Media *tepi*!'[3] they shout and shove me to the side. Sergeant Hamid Roslan gets into his car and we never see each other again.

At 4.15 p.m., I hover over Sharanjit's shoulder as he runs his eyes through my story. It is both, test and a teaching moment. He questions the veracity of my introduction. 'Are you sure she had a miscarriage? Bernama reported it as just an illness,' I explained myself with the evidence of scribbled notes and scratchy audio from my pocket recording. Sharanjit looks at me quietly before picking up the phone to seek reinforcement. Another editor arrives, Suresh, he speeds through the first three lines of my story and nods to Sharanjit. They confirm my success, and declare my story as worthy of being a lead on Page six.

Victorious, I slump into my seat, as my colleague swivels his chair over to offer me a vending machine treat, in exchange for my story about getting the story.

'Wah! Lucky you are a woman lah! Only women carry tissues in their bag!' my colleague chuckles before returning to his search for sources and story leads via their next-of-kin. The plane is still missing and 237 people remain lost. I do not feel lucky. I check my phone to find Tharish's reply to my pleas from hours ago, with a firm 'No. I'm sorry. I'm not the right person to give you this information.' I say that I understand. I do not feel lucky.

Sharanjit adds my byline to the front page and tells me to go home because labour laws won't allow me to stay. The guy I am seeing, texts to say we need to talk. We united at his house. I immediately gush about seeing my story in print and the front-page byline with my name alongside fellow esteemed journalists I looked up to. It was breathtaking. When I finish narrating about the wall I climbed, he brings up my sordid interaction with Tharish. My attempts of making his friend my source

---

[3]Translation: 'Members of the Media move aside! Move aside!'

was not well received. He liked me enough to explain to his friend that I was an enthusiastic rookie, under pressure to write a story. He apologized on my behalf but questioned my humanity:

'Don't you feel any remorse? Or sadness for the victims at all?'

He finds the answer in my body language, still giddy from winning and grief. I try to justify my compartmentalized compassion. That I genuinely cared for Sergeant Hamid Roslan. That I needed to capture a meaningful story. That I could hold both thrill and tenacity, at the same time. I wonder if male journalists are ever asked the same question, to prove if they have a heart. Are they ever questioned if they felt something when reporting on a tragedy? Or are they prized for being able to put their feelings aside?

We disappoint each other's expectations. I returned home to find my father awake at 6.15 a.m. It has been exactly twenty-four hours since we've both been recalled to work. Our house mimics a CNN Situation Room. Television and radio blaring the latest findings. Still no sign of the MH370. Over breakfast, my father and I dissected every newspaper, comparing the stories we caught and lost, to pre-empt the next lead we could chase. We pause from being father and daughter and rival journalists. We are equals, for a while.

My father weighs the morality of my journalistic choices and says he would have done the same. I feel validated until he tells me that I owe Tharish an explanation for my unkind line of questioning. He tells me that I have taken Tharish for granted. Being a journalist's source was never her role to play and meeting my deadline was never her burden to bear.

'She is not a journalist, she is the victim's best friend,' my father says.

I ponder over the possibility that being a good journalist and a good person might be mutually exclusive. My father interrupts my existential spiral with a reality check; the good thing and the right thing to do often exist in a gray area, without clear lines.

In the end, he says, the mark of a strong journalist is in their ability to capture complex emotions in ten sentences or less. I nod. He says, to record a moment of plight is to honour a piece of a person's history. I nod. He says, they are important even if they cannot see their significance right away. I nod at my father's industry-trained wisdom. It will take me seven years from this moment to acknowledge that it was more fuel than advice.

Fuel to keep chasing leads and make paragraphs out of people's lives. It is not bad advice if you want to succeed in the news business, but it is incomplete. There is a missing bridge between journalism and its ideas of success. Try as they might, college is hardly equipped to fulfill this gap, because in the fleeting moments of interviewing a distraught father or a best friend hanging onto a shred of hope, best practices do not apply. It is later reinforced by the industry, that the story always comes first. Success is granted to the piece that provokes emotion from the reader, not from the interviewee and never from the writer. My father is right and incomplete. With Tharish, I failed to be a journalist and a person but she succeeded in being a friend to her missing best friend. And that is the winning story, forever untold.

I return to the office before I am recalled again. It is day two of MH370 and theories begin to solidify on WhatsApp as ships are deployed to search the sea. Everyone knows nothing. The shock sinks in. More names and photos of passengers have surfaced. We now know who is on the plane but they might not be alive. Our grief and motivation are both renewed. Suresh is today's editor in charge. Yesterday's victory grants me today's blank page. He wants to know what story I have for him today but I am out of people to churn into sources. I offer no names. Suresh suggests I peek into the NST archives. This may be the first missing plane but it is not the first tragedy to befall the airline. I prepare to dig through history, to build a timeline of MAS mishaps, starting with the crash in Tanjung Kupang in 1977. Perhaps I will stumble upon a pattern of destruction, leading to my next story and maybe a follow up. I can see the headline now. Suresh picks up on the glee I try to hide. He smiles because it mirrors his own, 'Now is the best time to be a journalist, isn't it?'

The VIP Party of the Singapore F1 Grand PRIX

By Zulaiha Anjalika Kamis Gunnulfsen

'Babes, it's time to go.' I looked up and saw the face that I have grown very familiar with; my best friend, my partner in crime, my husband. We have just packed our bags, about to leave Norway for the umpteenth time, in the last ten years.

We are what you call expatriates. We have both been away from our respective countries for the last many years. Home is Kuala Lumpur, Malaysia for the last four years. Strange thing is that we are both very deeply rooted and hold so much love for our nations; his being Norway and mine, Singapore. Expatriatism has a strange way of making you feel more of who you are when away. I am a much prouder Singaporean than when I was living in Singapore—which had spanned more than two decades of my life and I know pretty much for sure Singapore will not be home anymore in the future. We have made plans to settle somewhere—few places come to our minds but Singapore was never one of them. As much as we both love the beautiful cosmopolitan island for obvious reasons like security, cleanliness and the easiness of doing business, the much obvious factor of high living costs makes the positives look pale in comparison.

It was while deep in these thoughts that I saw the flickering lights in my handbag, all packed and ready to go. Flickering lights in my bag could only mean one thing—someone at the other end of my smartphone was looking for me. I looked at the screen—it was my dear friend, Caroline from Singapore. Caroline is a friend who also heads one of the most prominent Public Relations firms in the Lion City. Almost immediately, my eyes rolled over to look at the clock on the wall—it is 4 a.m. in Singapore—what can be that important?

'Hey Car, what kind of story do you have to call me at this hour?'

'The kind of story I know you will be the best person for,' she chuckled. It was indeed a serendipitous moment because just as I was thinking about how proud I am as a Singaporean while being in the north pole, no less, that particular call was one that is going to make me cover one of the biggest events in Singapore. I was then the Editor, APAC for a regional marketing magazine.

The next couple of days, I was in a daze—excited, euphoric and nervous all rolled into one. Afterall, I am going to be covering a momentous event, one that has my city, Singapore buzzing with lights and action for a week, every year, close to a decade.

A week later, bags packed, I was on a flight out from Kuala Lumpur International Airport, heading south to Singapore. Flying on Singapore Airlines that day felt poignant—there is this undeniable pride that comes along, knowing I was going to be part of this huge international event, held in my beloved city, no less.

We had our first meeting at one of the bars in the city centre of Singapore.

When I first saw him, I cannot help but wonder how he managed to get this high-profiled position at such a young age. Tony Garrister is a well-built, tall, good-looking man, hailing from London. He is also down-to-earth, friendly and chatty. He has this undeniable aura that makes him stand out in the crowd. Tony runs the VIP entertainment segment of Formula One Races around the world—Dubai, Monaco, Italy and Singapore. He rubs shoulders with the likes of celebrities, sportspersons and ministers.

'Tell me, Tony, how did you get into this highly glamourized industry?' One of the very first questions I asked Tony.

'You need to love throwing parties and good ones too. From then on, build your brand using this flair that you have, get into the right company of people and never stop networking. You need to also be selective and conscious of those you are networking with. Like I always tell people—never underestimate the power of networking. Might seem like a silly small talk but it can help open doors otherwise you wouldn't even come close to' quipped Tony with his brilliant smile.

I have to admit, for someone who prides herself with being able to speak with anyone from all walks of lives, Tony did give me a little jitter; the kind that comes about when you are in the presence of someone so charismatic—the kind of feeling I always imagine to be feeling if I were ever to meet George Clooney!

Tony was busy that night, fleeting from table to table talking to patrons, most of whom he seemed to be familiar with. We talked about the upcoming event, the one that is going to be attended by celebrity racers and who's-who around the world. Just the sheer thought of how huge that is going to be, sent a chill down my spine—the good, the bad and the in-between kind of chill.

I flew back to Kuala Lumpur the next day to start preparing for the series. We agreed it was going to be a three-parter—an interview segment with Tony Garrister, Mr Founder himself. The second bit will be the event proper and the final part will be an after-event write-up. The more I researched, the more fascinated I became. The history, the people involved, the amount of money going around—it is just out of the world.

Ever since it started in 2008, the Singapore Grand Prix is one that has always been positively mentioned in the media all over the world. The island-nation's efficiency is the talk of racing officials and aficionados. In the meantime, Singaporeans do not seem too impressed with this yearly event taking their norms to disarray. Their day-to-day travelling routes, cordoned-off or they get rerouted, the city is packed with people from all over the world and traffic goes berserk that time of the year. I think this is such a small price to pay for global recognition and not to mention the spike in the economy especially for those in hospitality. I sometimes wonder if my fellow countrymen secretly revel the global attention their home country gets—if the naggings and complaints are just ways to get some conversations going amongst their peers. After all, the negatives usually get more attention than positives but one thing is for sure, I know I bask in this attention—everyone in the world, even those in the countryside of Italy know of this yearly phenomenon called the Singapore Grand Prix Night Race. Reminded me of the time I was in the rural bit of Italy in 2018 when a little lady, curious of this brown Asian girl wandering around her village, stopped, looked at me suspiciously—asked me in her heavily accented Italian where I am from. When I said 'Singapore', she flew her arms up in the sky and said, 'Ahhhhhh *la corsa notturna*!'

The Singapore Grand Prix week came. I was sleepless and highly excited. I flew into Singapore the night before the first race. A hotel close to the racetrack was home for the next three days, not having to stress and fuss about travelling to the event. The party was slated to be held in a five star hotel right next to the racetracks. Upon arrival, my heart jumped with pride. The whole Changi Airport atmosphere was magical; people laughing, chatting, excited about their weekend. I was beaming from ear-to-ear. The feeling of coming home to a place where the whole world will congregate gave an innate feeling of exuberance, words can never describe. The car ride from the airport gave me a lump in my throat, knowing if anything should happen anywhere in the world, this city—my city will always have my back.

I checked into the hotel, kicked off my shoes and started preparing for the big night. I was going to attend the first party of the season—the F1 kick-off party. A long white satin dress, strappy heels and a pair of dangly earrings was the ensemble of choice, not to mention my loyal work companion, a Canon DSLR.

Ready at 5 p.m., I went down to the hotel bar for some mocktails; it's a working night, mind you. I was not expected to be at the event ground until about 7 p.m. I was just soaking in the happy vibe in the bar when my phone buzzed. It was Tony wondering if I can make it over earlier. He's got someone he wanted me to meet. Picked up my bag and camera, called the driver that had been allocated to me by the organizers and made my way to the event ground. By now, my tummy has churned all over the place. I cannot help but wonder who Tony wants me to meet. I got to my destination in less than twenty minutes and after what seemed like a dozen of scannings and rounds of securities, I got into a huge hall—all decked in white. 'Perfect dress of choice, babes,' I said to myself. Ethereal came to mind.

At the far end of the hall, I spotted Tony and a gentleman chatting. He waved at me to come and join them. As I drew closer, I noticed a glass of Campari on-the-rocks each in their hands. The gentleman is of medium-built, tanned, hair slicked back and wearing a navy-coloured weekend suit. He smiled and at that moment, I realized I am in the company of someone very prominent in the F1 world. It was rather surreal. I had to blink hard a couple of times to confirm I was indeed in that moment, not just some crazy hallucination. We chatted, exchanged name-cards and promised to keep in touch.

Slowly people started coming in—a couple of expensive and impressive sports cars were on display. Lots of camera clickings—music got louder. I started seeing familiar faces—those you see on news, sports channels, theatres and movies. Everyone was in high spirits. I looked around, saw some people I know. Chatted a little while taking in everything around me—every so often something caught my attention and my camera clicked away. It marvels me how much people are willing to pay to get into these parties but then again, it is after all the place to see and be seen. On stage, a couple of world acts were serenading, dancing, gyrating, entertaining—keeping the audiences on their feet. I swayed my hips and body, joining in the party people.

For most people, drinks had taken effect and the merrymakers are now even chattier and merrier. They danced, they cheered, they partied as they had never partied before. The atmosphere was magical and I knew there is plenty to write about when I pen down my story.

It was midnight and the party did not seem to slow down - it got more intense—so intense that the bouncers of the night had to calm some down. From a distance, I saw a couple of faces of the race track walked in. They oozed an air of confidence and brilliance, one that you cannot miss—the kind you only see on those who have been to places many of us only wish we could. They were in high spirits, mingling and merrymaking with the crowd. The music was getting even louder, making it really hard for me to hold any conversations with anyone, let alone trying to have an interview-like chat with any of the racers. The energy was immense and the ambience was electric.

The party continued till the wee hours of the morning. The racers left earlier to catch-up on their sleep. They will have three days of gruelling competition ahead of them.

I left the scene close to 2 a.m. and even at that time, people were full-on drinking and mingling and laughing and moving to the music. Outside, many were waiting for their drivers or e-hailing services to come around. A couple of partygoers are now on the floor, purging every last bit of dinner and party snacks on the grass-patches. On my right, a well-dressed couple were arguing, no let's make that fighting. The fighting couple has often graced pages of Singapore high-society magazines. From the bits I was getting, apparently, in his wee-bit-drunk stupor, hit on a girl on the dance floor which left the Mrs in fury.

I smiled as I got into the car. The driver had been waiting for the last many hours while I was getting my story in the five-star property. He asked if I wanted to grab something to eat on the way back to the hotel. I declined the offer. At that point, I am just very happy the day is over—a fabulous one but I just cannot wait to return to my life; the one is waiting for me back in Kuala Lumpur and I also know there will be much to write about of this party.

Turning Lemons into Lemonade

By Nastasha Tupas

As I flipped my laptop closed to end what felt like the longest working day, the familiar sound of a notification bell prompted my iPhone to light up my makeshift, dimly lit home office. It has been a while, almost two years since I've ventured outside to work after Covid began and dictated the new normal.

Through the cracked display of my well-loved, battered iPhone screen, there was a message from my boss with a subject line that read 'contract end date'. After a solid three-and-a-half-year stint at this global, digitally driven media company, my time has come to an end. It's just the life of a contractor, right? I flipped my laptop back open to read that this ending was due to 'the changing needs of the business,' and the decision had nothing to do with my performance.

It felt a little like the 'it's not you, it's me' breakup scenario. The younger version of me, the newly minted wordsmith fresh out of college would have been absolutely gutted. In complete contrast, the current version of me—the slightly older and wiser version leaned in. If my eight-year tenure in the Australian media industry has taught me anything, is that there's no use fighting these things. It has already been decided. It never matters how much work you put in, how autonomous or efficient you are, how polished your video production is, how unique your articles are, or how many times your stories have been shared out there in the world of social media.

The past three years felt like I had put in more hours into work than I should have without taking home a single cent of overtime, diligently responded to after hours requests, shouldered a four-person job at a continually dwindling production team operating on a ridiculously perpetual shoestring budget without complaint. On top of all that, I had been producing original videos and writing articles to match. I have been a one-woman band and proudly wore many hats at this gig that's for sure, but, at the end of the day, three words can end three years of service—just like that. I'm having a hard time believing that the only reason is a 'change in direction'. I wonder what the actual culprit was this time around . . . Politics, the bamboo ceiling or a mixture of both? Who the fuck knows, I'm so over it at this point to be completely frank.

I'm not mad though, it is what it is. Dwelling on these things won't help. Why waste time and energy on what has already gone? Cutting loose, letting go and being decisive in planning the next move is key as to whether it's sink or swim. As clichéd as it may sound, there is always a better door opening-up after this one has locked itself shut. I take my glasses off and flip down my laptop screen because yeah, I'm totally done for today.

'Contract end date'. Those three words did get me thinking about why I romanticized working in the media back in high school anyway, even though the odds were not in my favour—especially because I wanted to be a TV presenter on a travel show. Years later, here we are, after finding out that media is not exactly a lucrative or a stable career, rolling contract after contract. It isn't as cool or glamorous as it seemed to that buck-toothed sixteen-year-old girl watching TV in Western Sydney.

If I could do it all again, I reckon I would have still followed along this path—I mean, to be completely frank, I was no good at science or maths despite the 'Asian centric' stereotype. I was that kid who almost never came up with the correct answer when singled out to respond to any kind of algorithmic query at Mr Frankston's mathematics class—if I did get any arithmetic right, it was most definitely a fluke, a straight-up one-hit-wonder.

But hey, I do love a good story though, whether I'm hearing one or telling one. The trouble is, anybody familiar with the Australian media landscape is guaranteed to notice that representation is limited even though the population is incredibly diverse. I guess I figured that out early-on. It would be a tall order to secure such a rare and coveted role such as a travel TV presenter in any circumstance, so I consciously pivoted into a career of video production and writing because I still get to tell stories from behind the camera.

There are five major free-to-air television channels here in Australia and that hasn't changed to this day. The TV channel of choice at my childhood home when I was a kid was this little multicultural public service broadcaster who had the Filipino news scheduled at 8 a.m. every day and had a wonderfully unique newsreader of south-east Asian descent on-air who read the local and national news every evening in fabulous fashion choices. Their presence as the country's flagship multicultural broadcaster made me feel like a serious career in media was possible growing up.

Fast forward to the foundational years of my media career, you can imagine how exciting it was for me when I got a letter of offer to start work as a digital producer and website editor at this multicultural network for a brand-new TV show. It wasn't smooth sailing though. I knew something was up when I swiped my pass to enter that newsroom hidden away in what seemed to be the building's basement, sans natural light, or a view outside. There seemed to be an unshakable air of melancholy. I couldn't put a finger on why that was, but it didn't take long for me to find out.

Just weeks into that new gig, it was apparent to me and every person in the small production team that the Executive Producer was a bully. Rumour had it that Australia's flagship, national public broadcaster had shown this Executive Producer the door after a decade as a journalist and on-camera talent due to the mounting bullying allegations by numerous staff, which meant that the elephant in the room could no longer be ignored. Based on the daily working life at the 'bunker,' that Executive Producer was working double-time to validate those rumours—same story, different TV channel.

A few of us in the team had nicknamed that Executive Producer 'The Trunchbull' or, 'The Trunch' for short, after the main antagonist in

Roald Dahl's 1988 novel, *Matilda*, because of how they carried on and seemed to enjoy the act of bullying others. Laughter ended up being the best medicine behind closed doors and acted as a coping mechanism for the trauma bonded production team who needed to hold on to the job despite the daily gaslighting, microaggressions and red flag after red flag that had popped up while working in conditions that took a very real and serious toll on mental health.

The quality of one's portfolio is important if one is serious about making it in media. As a junior journalist or producer, the main aim of the game is to build a well-curated portfolio that bears your byline because the quality and quantity of published work can determine how quickly your media career will take-off. Aspiring journalists and producers choose to hold on to shitty junior media jobs regardless of the red flags because a polished portfolio is the key to the next level up.

One of the Trunch's favourite pastimes was to move the goalposts on you. It didn't matter what kind of directive they gave to revise, or complete a task, the Trunch made sure issues were always guaranteed by the time sign-off came around even if their instructions were followed perfectly, to a tee. They also liked to get the production team together in a stuffy meeting room, each week to criticize, put-down, and shame each of us. They made sure each person in the team felt 'lesser than,' by the time the meeting was done.

None of those meetings were constructive or productive, ever, by the way. The Trunch offered no helpful feedback or insight about issues they took up with you. Most of the time, the Trunch just wanted to attack you for kicks not just in a professional sense but in a personal one too. Their agenda involved instigating and trapping you into circular conversations that were aimed at making you feel small. The Trunch wanted you to second guess, to crush your confidence, distrust judgment and betray yourself in such a stealthy, systematic, insidious fashion. The Trunch was clearly addicted to asserting their superiority and needed a constant hit, in locked echo-chambers, for their monstrous ego where nobody else's voice or view was allowed but theirs.

The other thing the Trunch enjoyed almost just as much as team meetings were ambush one-on-one meetings. They were the absolute worst. Expect a grilling session that can extend for over an hour, designed to make you feel afraid, nervous, anxious or upset, in a small, stuffy meeting room on the ground floor because the Trunch knew. They knew if there had been no witness, it would be their word against yours if you decide to report the instances of mental abuse, emotional abuse, gaslighting and intimidation. The Trunch must have really hated themselves if they were dependent on getting high, over thrills from terrorizing and mentally abusing other people . . . And, getting away with it for some kind of satisfaction.

It gets better though, the Trunch had been an aspiring movie star in their youth. I'd say they've got some passable 'acting' skills because they managed-up well and covered-up how they were systematically bullying their staff on a daily. With the advantage of a quarter of a century in broadcast media experience over the production team, the Trunch knew the shitty junior jobs they had on offer had an oversupply of applicants because any kind of broadcast television opportunity was few and far between. They were holding 'the proverbial carrot' which unfortunately, had given the Trunch and others like them, the unofficial license to terrorize young staff just because they KNOW they can.

That foundational gig was a wild ride for me. The nauseating rollercoaster finally came to a screeching halt because Human Resources was asked to step in after several, if not all the members in the production team, including myself, had asked for help after sitting through social, mental and emotional abuse. Those struggles shouldn't be happening in the workplace, period. Anyway, the result was astounding, the Human Resources team at that flagship 'multicultural' channel turned a blind eye to a middle-aged, Caucasian Executive Producer who had been blatantly using their position of power to openly oppress young ethnic staffers daily. In fact, that 'multicultural channel' cancelled all our contracts with as little notice as possible with the assistance of the same Human Resources department, immediately after production of the second season of the show had been completed. Yep, exactly the same 'Human Resources' team that did not care about staff well-being or concerns about systematic abuse because, surprise, surprise! Those two-faced bullshit artists were enablers, who were in on the corporate gaslighting ruse all along.

That television show went to air every week, celebrating inspiring migrant success stories—if only the audience knew of the heavy hearts that brought those stories to life behind the scenes, isn't it ironic? It only took that 'multicultural channel' several years to remove 'The Trunch,' but it wasn't because of the endless revolving door of staff, season after season. It only happened after the sponsorships ran dry, the ratings took a deep dive, and the show could no longer be resuscitated. Guess what? That isn't even the full story, a number of Indigenous Australians that formerly worked at that tragically Machiavellian 'multicultural' channel would have their own tales to tell about this particular topic.

No wonder most ethnic parents, namely Asian-Australian parents, try to veer their kids away from chasing a media or creative career of sorts. The approved 'safe' career paths include accounting, law, business, medicine, health or science, disciplines in industries deemed to be stable and secure. I once read an article that cited a study that found the average time an Aussie whose ethnic roots trace back to Asia gives a media career a 'proper crack' for a maximum of five years. That timeframe echoes my lived experience so far, but I thought I could do better and stick it out for another three years past that threshold. Yet, I've now found myself thinking of taking a break away from the commercial, mainstream media industry and maybe, tapping out altogether.

I was disappointed to say the least. I had never experienced anything like that growing up as a first-generation migrant in Australia during my schooling years, or at any of my previous non-media jobs . . . I remember feeling duped, I had never felt like I didn't belong somewhere until I began work in the media. That 'multicultural channel' had been playing ads about diversity, harmony and inclusion on repeat to a whole generation of migrants' kids like me. It was a very rude shock to discover that their 'inclusive' façade was just that—a façade and nothing more. Behind the scenes was not at all what their carefully curated public image had been implying for decades.

Most of us wouldn't sit through a bad relationship to protect our mental health and well-being, but for many in the industry, myself included, you start out telling yourself it won't be the same at the next gig. Until you realize by the time the fourth contract rolls to an end, it's always the same old pill just in different packaging.

Here's the thing, it starts from the top right? Those at the highest echelons dictate the company culture. Over the past few years, a worldwide movement championing representation, diversity and inclusion have seen a significant amount of momentum. For somebody permanently confined to the sidelines, it is a welcome change. There have been several interesting events throughout my career so far that legit had me thinking, 'what the fuck?!'

As I mentioned earlier, I had never experienced any kind of microaggression until I decided to follow this career path. After eight years in the industry and being immersed in many different newsrooms, I have been compelled to learn about 'the why,' so I decided to return to school. I've picked up a minor in Psychology to help me make more sense of my lived experiences and what I have seen and heard so far.

I have so many questions. Like why the industry in my home country hasn't invested well-enough in representing the diverse Australians that watch national television, read the newspapers, consume online media and flick through glossy magazines? Why do microaggressions that happen within media corporations fly under the radar or outright overlooked? How and why did these newsroom environments become so toxic and mentally hostile? Why do these media corporations enable bullying and back the bullies instead of supporting the victims? Perhaps it's easier to turn a blind eye to it all and sweep it under the rug.

It really is food for thought. I suspect part of it could be the longstanding, harmful stereotypes. You know the ones I'm talking about—the subservient perception of Asian women, is one that could have heavily influenced a number of questionable experiences I've had so far. That perception alone is damaging in so many ways because it distastefully empowers exploitative colleagues and organizations to treat you as if you're invisible, of lesser value to a team or easily disposable no matter how much focus and dedication you invest in your work.

Damaging perceptions like this one, pigeonholes an entire group as 'just the worker,' and never the manager that can lead or strategize. The reserved but thoughtful demeanour is almost always misconstrued as feeble and vapid when it is very much the opposite—it's always 'the empty can' that makes the loudest noise. Funnily enough, the industry seems to value the latter purely based on the level of noise and how far up it notches on the decibel scale.

Sometimes, ideas you share via 'collaborative' brainstorming sessions get written-off but mysteriously debut as branded, premium digital video products months after the discussion, a moneymaking machine wholly credited to the senior colleague that blatantly dismissed the same idea in the first place. Of course, it can never be an idea you came up with because you're just the 'worker', right?

Don't get me started on the countless 'sit back down' moments after you put your hand up or pitch to chase story opportunities but get overlooked and constantly passed over by the 'leadership team' every single time due to unconscious bias courtesy of the stereotype that has dictated the 'driver's seat is not for you, it will never be for you' purely because of what you look like and where your parents immigrated from.

Oh, if you're lucky, pitching diverse, inclusive and community representative content will also be knocked back, outright ignored, buried in the depths of the company platforms or excluded from the social media channels simply because, quote, 'that isn't for our audience', despite what Sydney city streets and neighbourhoods look like in 2021.

Here's the other thing. Management can choose to pick up the slack to change the narrative by making room for diverse, inclusive, and representative stories. The reasoning behind the tired, old 'that's not for our audience' spiel is absolutely redundant and such a beat-up when the main offerings at some of these places are clickbait en masse for some lols, shits, and giggles but packaged up as 'news delivered differently'.

It's really interesting that the decision makers are called the 'leadership team'. Where is the demonstrated 'leadership' when the decisions made are constantly designed to exclude? Where is this 'leadership' without empathy and accountability? Where is the 'leadership' at tone-deaf mass communication conglomerates that fail to fairly understand, support and amplify underrepresented voices? Where is the 'leadership' in refusing to see the world in colour?

Apparently investing any time and resources into producing original stories that matter, meaningful and engaging content that informs, or delivering stories that are representative of the diverse Australian audience is just not worth it because that stuff belongs at the small-scale ethnic community channels. Commercial channels and platforms don't have room for that, because it belongs in the 'too hard basket,' so really, the underlying message there is, nope, no room for people like you. Of course, nobody ever says that out loud because it's not PC these days, it'll most likely result in a PR emergency and will undo any lip service these media companies have invested marketing money in. It's all about keeping up appearances, it's not about actual leadership that addresses the status quo with constructive contributions via strategies aimed at making real, impactful, sustainable change.

Honestly, it has been exhausting having to push against the double standards, unconscious bias and unbelievable lack of support. It's no wonder silence and self-preservation are preferable at this point. It has, unfortunately, become the 'go to' and after eight years, it's time to go, take these lemons and make some refreshing lemonade. Fuck it.

Luckily, there are many ways storytellers can back themselves and thrive on digital platforms these days without having to endure another day, sitting through yet another 'collaborative' meeting which really is just another phishing session in disguise. No thanks, I'm done with that too.

I'll still be a storyteller, that's for sure. As this chapter of my career ends, I'm looking forward to what is next with excitement and optimism because as the saying goes, 'A bird sitting on a tree is never afraid of the branch breaking, because her trust is not on the branch but on her wings.'

The Motel Editor

By Caitlin Liu

I was probably eleven years old when I edited someone for the very first time.

I know I couldn't have been older as it happened when my family was living at El Patio Motel, before we moved a block down Highway 86 to our third motel home, where I turned twelve.

The recipient of my first editing work was my father. His audience: the city government of El Centro, population 23,000 in the heart of Imperial Valley, the southeastern flats of California where much of America's lettuce, broccoli, and alfalfa are grown. The city had sent my father a letter regarding our family's motel. Something about needing a permit—for what, I can no longer recall. My father wanted to explain, in writing, why a permit was not needed, but English was hard for him. He grew up speaking German with his mother and Mandarin with his father. He learned to read and write only in Chinese at the many schools he passed through in mainland China and then in post-war Taiwan. In America, his home of five years, the words my father wanted to say to the City of El Centro kept tumbling out wrong.

My father handed me a sheet of notebook paper filled with handwritten words. Some were crossed out. Some were scribbled in the margins. He explained to me, in Mandarin, what he wanted to say to the City of El Centro.

I pecked out my father's intentions on a manual typewriter while correcting his spelling and grammar along the way.

* * *

I sometimes trace the start of my obsession with the English language to that day, when I began editing my father's writing, inside that small living room with rose-patterned carpeting behind the front counter of El Patio Motel. The letter I edited persuaded the city government that my father was correct, and no costly repair work would be needed. My editing helped protect my parents' business that was also our family home.

It would dawn on me later: Language is power. Language is armour. Language is not the kingdom, but surely one of its keys.

But if you had to ask anyone, when I was a child, what I would become one day, working as an editor professionally as I do now and being looked to as a master over the written language—in English, no less—would not have come to mind.

As a child in Taiwan, I had no special love of the Chinese language. If anything, I found language learning to be rather painful. I had been writing Chinese characters over and over again for homework since I started school at three years old. At age four, I had so much daily written homework that I had no time for my father when he came home for a visit, his ship back to the port of Keelung after months away at sea for his maritime industry job. When I was six, if my classmates and I could not recite correctly the passages we were supposed to memorize from our textbook, the teacher would march over to our scruffy wooden desks to hit us over the head with her bamboo stick.

Later, my father would tell me that he and my mother decided to leave Taiwan and move our family to America because they wanted my brother and me to have a different kind of education.

* * *

My journey to America began on 1 July 1976, the opening day of the new freeway between Keelung and Taipei.

I sat with my mother and brother in the back of a family friend's shiny black sedan, speeding to Taipei's airport in record time, so we could finally join my father in America, where he had already been living for a year. My grandparents and other relatives followed in a separate car. At the airport, we took photos and said goodbyes.

As I lined up behind my mother and little brother to enter a pre-boarding area, I looked back and saw my grandmother's face in the crowd.

That morning, she had brushed tangles out of my long hair. I was wearing a white blouse with a fancy collar and red plaid bell-bottom overalls that she had sewn. My grandmother looked ashen. I turned away quickly to resume moving forward, so I wouldn't cry.

My first airplane ride, between the little island we left behind and the big new world to come, was uneventful. I slept across three seats, head on my mother's lap, while my brother curled up on the carpeted floor. At Los Angeles International Airport, a man with large pork chops for sideburns, a shy smile, and a face I didn't quite recognize strode over to us.

His arms wrapped around my brother and me for a long time. I knew he had to be my father, but he felt like a stranger. My arms didn't know what to do so they hung stiffly at my sides. As my head squished against this person who was my father, my face turned to watch other people at the terminal walking by.

My father put our suitcases into the back of a white Chevy Corvair. Within minutes of pulling out of the airport, down Century Boulevard, the Corvair puttered into the driveway of our first American home—a motel where my mother would soon join him at work.

* * *

In America, nothing was familiar. My first pizza made me vomit. Our TV dazzled with thirteen channels—ten more than Taiwan. During my first ever visit to a supermarket, I broke out in goosebumps from the cold.

I watched my father, a former merchant marine officer, sweep cigarette butts from our motel driveway as my former schoolteacher mom pushed a maid's cart piled high with linens and toilet paper.

Before we left Taiwan, someone taught me how to recite the English alphabet. Once in America, I realized I did not know the twenty-six letters out of order or arranged in different combinations. Aside from my new English name, I did not know other English words.

But the alphabetic chaos all around me mellowed quickly, as letters began organizing into formation and units of understanding: *Apple Jacks* was breakfast. *Safeway* makes me shiver even though it's summer. At *ARCO*, gas costs fifty cents a gallon. *Sesame Street* and *Winchell's glazed donuts* were my new favourite things ever.

Two months after I arrived in Los Angeles, my father brought me to my first American school.

Inside the principal's office, a tall man with a toothy smile and penchant for enunciating every word bent down to me:

'Caaaaan youuuu spellll Califorrrniaaaahh?'

I could not. But I almost joked, 'C-A'—as that was what I saw my mother write as part of her return address on all her Aerogram letters to her parents in Keelung. But I also remember thinking that a wisecrack like that might not go over well at this first meeting with an important person. So I said nothing.

That was that. Though I had already finished second grade at the top of my class in Keelung, Mr Cordell said I needed to start in second grade in Los Angeles.

Later at home, I asked my dad how to write 'California'. He wrote 'Ca' on a sheet of paper before, at my insistence, revealing in a pained script the remaining eight letters. I committed California, in its full ten-letter glory, to memory that same day.

* * *

If Mr Cordell made me pay closer attention forevermore to English spelling, Mrs Thompson surely deserves credit for my literary awakening.

Inside Mrs Thompson's second grade classroom, a wonderland in technicolour compared to the dusty browns and grays of my Taiwanese school, I read my first English book, *A Rainbow of My Own* by Don Freeman. I was also introduced to the mysterious disconnects between English as spoken and English that is seen. Rules were rules, until they weren't. The *foo* in *food* looks just like but is not supposed to sound like the *foo* in *foot*.

One day, Mrs Thompson announced a special word game: coming up with homophones. Two of her five classroom aides, Mrs Frost and Mrs Yogi, affixed a large paper tree to a classroom wall.

Mrs Thompson invited everyone to come up with words that sound the same but are spelled differently. Every new word pair or trio would cause the tree to 'sprout' new fruit—a paper pear cutout bearing those identical-sounding words. Like pear, pair and pare.

As more and more paper pears bearing word pairs grew on
Mrs Thompson's tree, I grew more and more excited. I could not come
up with any word pairs of my own, but I went to that tree every day for
my own secret harvest.

In bed at night, as other children counted sheep, I could only think
about Mrs Thompson's word game and what I saw on that tree: *Toe, tow.
Blue, blew. Sunday, sundae. By, buy . . . bye.*

My daily consumption of Sesame Street and its skits on phonics
kicked off another bedtime mental parade:

Bat . . .

Cat . . .

Fat . . .

Hat . . .

Mat . . .

I began devouring the English language gluttonously and
indiscriminately, and I foraged everywhere.

No cereal box, store display or street sign escaped my hungry eyes.

I eagerly awaited our postman, who might have well been Santa for
showering me daily with all kinds of new words. I puzzled over Publishers
Clearing House sweepstakes rules and tried to decipher offers from
Columbia House Record Club. My mother was learning how to drive, and
I read every page of her California Department of Motor Vehicles traffic
rules manual so many times that I took a practice written test and passed.

* * *

It was only years later, to my surprise, that I heard people older and
much more learned than I describe the English language as expressive,
versatile and even beautiful. But for me, English was survival. My urge
to gorge on every English word in sight was probably not too different
from how a starving animal might treat anything remotely edible within
pouncing distance.

To this day, I get excited about new words. I also feast with reckless
abandon, sometimes forgetting time and forgoing sleep, on the good
writing of others. My hunger for words is so visceral, so all-consuming
that sometimes digesting the same string of words just once is not enough.

I have read and reread passages from Toni Morrison and Gabriel Garcia Marquez, Milan Kundera and Dave Eggers, so pleasurable is the musicality of their writing. Graydon Carter's acerbic editor's notes for *Vanity Fair* exerted on me similar black magic—the urge to replay him again and again. More recently, it was Nate White—that Brit of rapier wit whose essay on Trump I have read from top to bottom three times, the first two times in a row. Even though, each time, it hurt a little, because the immigrant child in me, the one who has long learned to overedit herself in the presence of people like my second-grade principal, now knows full well the difference between *being in command of* the English language and the swagger of *owning* the English language. The latter is the birthright I do not have.

But if I had been born into the English language, I might have taken it for granted, as I still do with my Chinese.

* * *

Journalists communicate. Journalists reveal. We like to uncover secrets and tell the world all. But the journalist's own self is another matter.

Through most of my adult life and journalism career, it wasn't so much that I would lie about my English-as-a-second-language, childhood-in-motels background. I simply did not talk about it. To this day, some of my closest friends do not know.

Right or wrong, I sensed that pedigree seemed important to the kind of world I was entering, and a fancy dog I was not. Connections and access were highly valued, and I had none. But native English fluency—that most basic of an American journalist's qualifications— was something I was able to fake without misrepresenting anything on paper.

At one former employer, a mentor advised me to be more humble, to keep my head down, because there were people who saw me as 'silver spoons' and felt resentful. I had been hired through a training program intended for minorities and the disadvantaged—so what was someone like me doing there? Perhaps my Stanford diploma and polished work wardrobe—the best that my student loan budget could afford from thrift stores—sowed class confusion. Or maybe it was my periodic lapses into what might have sounded like lily white 'Valley Girl' speech intonations. Though, if one listened carefully, my Valley speak was not of the Moon Unit Zappa's privileged San Fernando variety but from farther inland, deeper south and much more hardscrabble Imperial.

No matter. I was mistaken as a member of the ruling class. The motel child in me exulted!

The kid who once spoke no English, qualified for free lunch and had parents whose daily labors included unclogging toilets and changing bedsheets soiled by others, had cracked the class code in one of America's most prestigious, hardest-to-get-hired-into newsrooms. I was 'passing'.

* * *

Whenever someone asked about my journalism and editing qualifications, I would try to speak what I believed was their language, using code to convey what I thought they valued and wanted to know.

I was an editor at The *Stanford Daily* and editor-in-chief of The *Citizen*, a Harvard Kennedy School newspaper. I trained through a Dow Jones editing program and an editing apprenticeship at the *New York Times*. For most, that's usually more than enough information.

What I didn't bother to tell, because time is short I honestly didn't think most people had the interest, is where I really cut my teeth as an editor—for my parents' motel business.

After my typewritten handiwork helped keep the City of El Centro inspectors at bay, my father awarded me more editing and writing jobs. For a stretch, I was also the motel sign maker.

A motel is a little world unto itself, a mini-civilization with myriad rules that, if broken, can really mess things up. Guests need to know what to do and not do. Where to go and where they must stay out of. Open hours for the coin laundry room need to be posted, as does a reminder on the dryer to clean the lint screen before use. Parents of small children must be warned that there is no lifeguard on duty at the swimming pool.

Making a good sign is not too different from crafting a good headline for SEO. To reach the greatest audience, it's best to use words that are simple and popular. As a motel sign-maker, I used stencils of different sizes, planning and adjusting spacing between letters and numbers, to make all the words fit within the allotted space in a visually attractive manner. Unnecessary words, words that cluttered, would be cut out.

These days, for my job as an editor for an English language news platform based in Hong Kong, I use Google Docs to size up and resize headlines, deleting unnecessary verbiage, to make the words fit better and their meaning clearer. I also correct broken grammar and rewrite as needed, to better convey what I think are the writer's intentions.

I try not to think too much about questions that are unanswerable. What would I have become if my family hadn't left Taiwan, or if my parents had emigrated earlier and I had been able to acquire English more easily and naturally from birth?

What if my father had remained a supermarket security guard—his first job after he landed in America—rather than deciding he would try to make a better living by going into business for himself, which resulted in my childhood in a succession of motels? Would being the daughter of a security guard rather than an innkeeper have propelled me into a similar career?

I don't let myself stay in those mental spaces for long not because it's too difficult, but because the answer almost doesn't matter. I have been editing others for a very long time, and it feeds me amply—though the pangs of longing when I read the gorgeous writing of others will likely always be there.

A Cambodian Love Affair

By Marissa Carruthers

'But there's a war going on.'
'It's dangerous.'
'How will you get electricity?'
This is just a handful of statements I received from friends and relatives when in 2012 I dropped the bombshell that I was quitting my dream job of a decade working at a bustling daily newspaper in the UK, putting the dream home I'd spent years making my own on the market and leaving behind everything I'd ever known to move to Cambodia.

I'd visited the country the previous year during my first jaunt to Southeast Asia and, to be fair, I arrived with pretty much the same preconceptions. We don't hear much about Cambodia in the UK. I doubt many could even point it out on a map—*somewhere near Thailand, I guess?* For those who lived through the 1970s, hazy memories of Pol Pot and war occasionally hitting the headlines may be stirred. For everyone else, poverty . . . oh, and maybe, Angkor Wat.

I too had naively expected to land in a semi-warzone dogged by dire poverty. Of course, I'd done my research—planning's all part of the adventure, right?—but the internet is a fool's game and all searches seemed to flash up was a long history of suffering and not much else.

The human atrocities, genocide, death and destruction endured during the Khmer Rouge reign. Refugees fleeing across the border to Thailand in the hope of finding new lives in France, America, Australia, whoever would have them. A country trying, and seemingly failing, to rebuild itself after decades of turmoil.

Then there was the poverty porn. In all its droves. Backpackers posing next to malnourished kids with faces caked in dirt. Groups of travellers crouched alongside street children, naive 'do-gooders' at an orphanage among youngsters wearing wide grins and throwing peace signs at the camera. Shots of trash pickers and their children drowning in oceans of waste.

Combined, these two factors paint a very strong picture of Cambodia to the unacquainted eye. So, when in 2011, I landed in the capital after a trip around Thailand, I was more than pleasantly surprised. In fact, the cliché I'd spent my career avoiding—'city of contrasts'—suddenly seemed very apt.

Battered Honda Dreams spewing out smog wove in and out of gleaming Lexus. Sprawling communities of tin-roofed huts sat in the shadows of skyscrapers in the midst of construction. Hoarding boasting the entry of lauded international brands shrouded the countless building sites that dotted the city. Change physically and metaphorically hovered on the horizon. I could feel its very essence lurking in every nook and cranny. It felt exciting; a diamond in the rough.

As I travelled across the country, again and again I was amazed by the kindness of the Cambodians I met. Vann, my tuk-tuk driver at the temples—now a firm friend—invited me to his family home for dinner, giving me my first glimpse into local life. Sinet beckoned me to his table one night at a restaurant and we spent hours cheering and chatting over beers. Sophea, a then twenty-seven-year-old waitress, offered to show me around the capital and introduced me to some of her journalist friends. Little did she know this would be a life-changing event. As I spoke to the Khmer, American and Australian journalists, I knew I wanted to follow in their footsteps and in my head started planning my move.

Of course, that isn't to say these issues don't exist. Poverty is rife across Cambodia and the aftermath of the Khmer Rouge reign hangs heavy in the air like oppressive monsoon skies. Outside Phnom Penh sit only a handful of urban hubs—Siem Reap, Battambang, Kampot—but even they have a small town-like feel.

The remainder of the country is rural. A swathe of the predominantly agricultural population lives on less than one dollar a day and the nation is dogged with a raft of social, environmental and political issues. Corruption, gender inequality, illegal logging and the decimation of ancient rainforests, sand dredging, land grabbing, illegal wildlife trafficking, political crimes. The list goes on and on and on.

But what stood out to me during my short trip was a country teetering precariously on the brink of change and a new generation demanding something different. It was this, along with Cambodia's rich culture, heritage and history that sits on the opposite end of the spectrum to my life in England, that lured me in. I felt like the rest of the world was being fed an illusion, that there is much more to the complex Cambodia I was drawn to than the negative image being portrayed internationally.

***

Less than a year later, on a dank October day back in 2012, I stood in Newcastle International Airport's departures terminal armed with a suitcase, a one-way ticket to Cambodia and about US$800 in my bank account. Tears streamed down my cheeks as I bid my sister farewell and waited in the check-in queue.

Pangs of doubt poisoned the mind that had previously been preoccupied with the excitement of a new life abroad, building up a portfolio of international work as a first-time freelancer, expanding my horizons.

Suddenly, reality smacked me in the face like a sack of cement. I had no job waiting for me on the other side. No contacts. I'd never even sent a pitch to an editor, having spent my career as a full-timer working on newspapers. No friends. No real clue about life in Cambodia or its culture. How to find a house. How to navigate this new, unknown world I was a total stranger to . . .

I mean, will I actually have electricity? What if there is still a war going on I was unaware of?

What in the actual fuck am I doing?

***

While blackouts were commonplace across the capital in 2012, I did have access to electricity and it didn't take me long to settle into my new home-away-from-home. Excitement quickly replaced fear as I greedily soaked up the smells, sights and sounds of the bustling metropolis.

As a melting pot of cultures with a strong expat scene, Phnom Penh thankfully turned out to be an easy city to navigate as a stranger. It didn't take long to make friends thanks to a vibrant social scene, and finding a house was as simple as driving around on the back of a moto in search of 'for rent' signs.

I frantically set about familiarizing myself with Cambodia and the media landscape, scouring the local news and quizzing locals and expats about life in the aptly-named *Kingdom of Wonder*. Within a couple of weeks, I started to nervously fire off my first ever blind pitches.

My background was in hard news but I soon discovered there was no shortage of foreign journalists working in this field. Back then, we were blessed with a stalwart crew of seasoned foreign correspondents who had been flying in and out since the 1990s and a relatively independent media in the form of the *Phnom Penh Post* and *Cambodia Daily*—both of which were shuttered ahead of the 2018 general elections in a raft of measures that saw Cambodia stripped of its independent media, but that's a story for another chapter.

I quickly managed to muscle my way into the role of deputy editor at one of the country's leading lifestyle magazines. Fluff is what my hard news mind initially dismissed this as, remembering how us news journalists at my former paper would snobbishly look down our noses at the features desk, seeing ourselves as far superior. However, this turned out to be my calling, and the door to finding the positive stories I yearned to write.

'I became bored of reading negative stories about Cambodia,' the publisher barked during a casual chat we had ahead of me starting. He moved to Cambodia in 2005 after a few-year stint in Vietnam. Even back then, it seemed he'd quickly grown bored of the same mantra as me.

Deciding to plug a gap in a then-burgeoning media landscape, he launched a magazine that celebrated the country's change-makers. That examined emerging trends and movements, primarily spearheaded by Cambodia's huge young population. That threw the spotlight on the plethora of positives emerging from this almost-forgotten corner of the globe.

I grabbed the contract and scrawled my signature on the dotted line.

***

People often ask me why I became a journalist. There are many reasons. Since a child, I've had an insatiable curiosity for the world around me—a polite way of saying I'm inherently nosy. I'd annoy my parents with my constant barrage of questions and, unsatisfied with the answers, seek out alternative sources to verify what they said.

I also bore easily. The very thought of being chained to a desk like a battery hen, churning out the same mundane tasks day in and out sends chills down my spine. Then there's my activist side; something I seem to have grown up with. I remember as a child in the eighties the feeling of sheer helplessness as pictures of Ethiopians ravished by the famine flashed up on the TV. This side of me wants to expose injustice, raise awareness about untold or ignored issues and tell stories that bring about change, however miniscule, to the world. Additionally, there's my lifelong love of writing and documenting my surroundings—just ask my parents about the piles of notebooks I'd amass as a child.

As a rookie reporter, I quickly realized the incessant probing that irritated my loved ones was actually an asset. Boredom also wasn't something I needed to fear in my career. Besides deadlines preventing any form of office clock-watching from setting in, boredom was staved off by the adrenaline rush of sniffing out exclusives to secure the next day's splash, chasing stories ahead of my competitors, meeting a multitude of different people and digging deep into a range of topics depending on what that particular day's news dealt.

But most importantly, I discovered what drives me in journalism is the privilege of being able to tell other people's stories, immerse myself in alternative worlds, view life differently through another set of eyes. It was my job that gave me a gateway to really discover Cambodia and all her complexities; a journey that continues to this very day.

***

As my one-year anniversary hurtled towards me, the whims of returning home faded. The adrenaline rush that had fed me back in the newsroom was replaced with fascination. My curiosity had sparked another insatiable thirst, this time to learn more about this country I was falling in love with. I decided to stick around a little longer to ride the tide of change that was brewing and renewed my visa for another year.

Through interviews with master dancers, hypnotized by the majestic moves that once enchanted Angkorian kings, I fell in love with Cambodian ballet—or Apsara. I learned about the struggle of emerging modern artists trying to break away from the shackles of tradition and paint Cambodia in a contemporary light. I was constantly humbled by the determined efforts of a generation of young Cambodians fighting for the future of their country, whatever the cost.

Over the next few years, I climbed the ladder to editor and saw Cambodia at her best and worst. I spent lavish nights in whatever latest luxury hotel was opening and devoured the food of whichever Michelin star chef had been flown in that particular month. I attended endless openings. Red carpet events. Rubbed shoulders with the rich and famous.

I travelled deep into the provinces and witnessed abject poverty, squalor that made my heart ache. I spent nights in the jungle accompanying rangers on their deadly patrols and walked alongside mahouts and their elephants as they trudged through Mondulkiri's rolling jungle. I ventured deep into the heart of Southeast Asia's largest intact rainforest, the Cardamom Mountains, to release endangered animals rescued from the clutch of illegal poachers back into the wild. I slept on the dusty wooden floors of countless family homes in the countryside and made many firm friends along the way.

I've been inspired time and time again by a young generation of innovators who are spearheading changes in health, education, women's rights, equality, technology. I've left interviews in awe of the strength and passion of activists who risk their lives to protect their freedom and fight for democracy. A fight that can easily end in jail or death, as it has already for many.

In spite of the unimaginable hardships I encountered, the frustration and the injustice, there was always some form of hope shining through the people I interviewed.

***

'I'm fed up of hearing about the Khmer Rouge,' sighed a twenty-two-year-old Cambodian researcher I was interviewing for a story I was writing entirely hooked on the Khmer Rouge. Having won a scholarship to study in the UK, she recalled her time in London. 'Every time I told someone I was from Cambodia, I'd hear something about the Khmer Rouge.'

And it wasn't just her. The feeling was so strong among her peers that she went on to write her thesis examining how Khmer Rouge narratives shape millennial Cambodians' identity.

'Yes, it's important we never forget, the country is still healing, but my generation, the second generation, didn't live through it. That's not Cambodia any more. We want to create our own legacy, not be constantly tied to the past. We want the world to see us as Cambodia, not the Khmer Rouge.'

After four years as editor, I had decided to venture into full-time freelancing. While finding a way to focus on the positive on home turf was relatively easy, on an international scale it's tough. We all know bad news sells, alongside doom, gloom, death, misfortune and violence. How strangely macabre is the human mind?

Seemingly, the only avenue to sell stories was to hook them to the Khmer Rouge, reaffirming the very rhetoric a generation was trying to escape. A story about the country's first female punk rocker; the first LGBT Apsara dance troupe; emerging music, biking, art, skating scenes; even martial arts. Each editor demanded a Khmer Rouge reference at least. Otherwise some reference to poverty, despair, violence. Each time audience intrigue was cited as justification.

I explained this to my interviewee, a wave of shame washing over me. Was I just another foreigner trying and failing to tell stories that aren't mine to tell in a country that will never truly be home? She kindly reminded me my job was to give a voice to the voiceless and provide them with a platform to shout their message to whoever may be listening.

In spite of this, this is a question that still haunts me every now and again as I now hurtle towards my nine-year anniversary in Cambodia—a place that I can now truly call my home-away-from-home as England's familiarity fades away. However, I continue to try and promote the positive, even if it has to be wrapped in shades of grey. I continue to learn daily—about Cambodia and myself—and I continue to be ever-grateful to journalism for giving me all of the opportunities and life experiences it has.

Getting Teargassed
Was No Fun

By Reta Lee

I'd say I never had any formal training in news reporting, but I had a knack for reporting news if you get what I mean. It's about delivering content that people want, and sometimes you have to nudge them towards something they'd be interested in reading.

Malaysian politics was at the cusp of a people's revolution around 2011. Or so, I'd like to think. I was never really interested in politics, let alone did I vote in the last election. Terrible, I know. But soon, all of that was to change. When you're programming news for a major digital platform, you can't help but take a personal stance after reading and researching. The economy was breaking down; reports of high-price goods to increasingly dangerous crimes in the streets and corruption were the headlines of the dailies every day.

I hired Kenneth, my now-ex boyfriend, as my temp videographer. I knew he had the skills to edit and shoot, and I needed someone who could provide a quick work turnaround. Also, he got heavily involved with on-ground activism, which provided me with some insights to a couple of non-governmental organizations.

By then, I signed up as part of a small news coalition group, that counted news organizations such as *Malaysiakini*, *The Rocket* and other independent news sites such as Malay Mail and more. We sometimes group once or twice a week outside *Malaysiakini's* office in Bangsar, just discussing and sharing resources. Of course, there would be a table of plainclothes men just around the corner, enjoying their hot milk tea and roti canai.

I felt *invisible*.

I felt like I was doing my part for the country, being involved from the grassroots, and delivering the truth to our readers. There was never a time that I felt threatened.

I continued to attend the political parties' talks from one state to neighbouring towns.

And I was especially drawn to Ambiga Sreenevasan, the chairman of Bersih, or known as Coalition for Clean and Fair Elections, a coalition made up of sixty-two non-governmental groups aimed to draw attention and importance to Malaysia's state, namely in the last elections' tampering. As a lawyer, she was strong, independent, yet motherly. She even received the International Women of Courage Award, an American award presented for those who showed leadership, courage and resourcefulness, and championing women's rights. There she was, a pivotal female figure taking on the monsters of our beloved country!

When Ambiga speaks into the mic, her voice punctures through even the slightest doubt in your mind. My eyes caught hers a couple of times during her live speeches at rallies, and they radiated goodness, like a wise person's. I've never cared for politics but with her speeches, she draws you in and you'd simply feel unbreakable. What a remarkable feeling to have!

I also felt her kindness. She would stop and spend some time just talking to people who come up to her, even if it's just a simple 'hello'. Over the years I've come to appreciate her strength, kindness and dedication—traits I'd like to think I've instilled in myself, should I become a leader one way in the organization I work for.

As the talks and protests gained momentum, Bersih announced a large scale street protest in September 2011, demanding the government to fulfil their eight demands, like cleaning the electoral roll, reforming the postal ballot to stopping corruption. A street protest! I've never attended one before, and something inside my core shook; as an individual, by participating in one, I felt like being part of something this big, *maybeeee* I could make a difference. As a journalist, capturing this visually on camera and paper has to be the riskiest job in journalism. I don't have experience being on the road, let alone protecting myself should things go south. But I'm needed more than ever.

I prepped my editorial team for a significant coverage—from liveblogging coverage, to photo galleries. With a small team and lack of resources, I doubled as the photographer. The night before D-day, Kenneth had already researched how to neutralize tear gas.

Was it *even* necessary? I didn't take him seriously as I watched him shook baking soda with water in a bottle.

Maybe he knows something I don't know.

The eve of the protest, Kenneth and I took my car, parked it nearby enough for us to get it, and walked into town. The police had earlier barricaded Merdeka Square and her surrounding environment. The square was where our Father of Independence Tunku Abdul Rahman signed the treaty, making Malaysia an independent state from the British. Ambiga chose the square as it was the square for all Malaysians to come together and share. It had a loud message, and the ruling government was having none of it.

I can still remember that evening clearly; we fed our furkids early, ensuring the house we shared at Taman Seputeh was okay and joined fellow activists in front of Bar Council on Leboh Pasar Besar. It felt like a large festive gathering; so many chatter lifted spirits, smiles all around. All races congregated together, and our skin colour, race and culture made who we are so unique as Malaysians. And we were all here to make our voices heard.

'Do you think there will be hundreds of people tomorrow?'

'Maybe thousands, perhaps larger than the other street protests Bersih had kicked off since 2007,' one of the activists shared.

Kenneth made the call to stay overnight, and I followed suit.

I laid on the tarred road, with my backpack as my pillow looking at the stars as midnight crept close. I probably tweet or Facebook this as my caption before. And friends replied, 'to be careful'.

We observed the special forces watching us with barb wires surrounding us and a heavy-armed SWAT-like presence. *Was this necessary? Wouldn't they want to fight for their country too?*

Kenneth scribbled 'Welcome to Tel Aviv', and with a grin on his face, he stuck it on the razor fence. I watched him as he smirked, its message clearly pointing to the similar state we were in, to Israel. The irony, come to think about it.

My face drew a worried expression: *Would a cop jump on him? Would he immediately get arrested?* I quickly brushed that notion aside; after all, we were already partaking in a street protest deemed illegal by the government. Any concerns disappeared to where the wind blows.

Little would we know, that stupid A4 slogan paper of his appeared in pictures of major dailies worldwide, including a blog post written by former Prime Minister Mahathir Mohamad's daughter Marina. Kenneth had the smuggest face for days and I confessed to him, it was a pretty rad, if not ballsy move. I wouldn't have the same guts to do what he did. Furthermore, as I was playing my role as a journalist first, citizen second, I made sure to observe and make notes of my surroundings.

Kenneth had the smuggest face for days and I confessed to him, it was a pretty rad, if not ballsy move. I wouldn't have the same guts to do what he did. Furthermore, as I was playing my role as a journalist first, citizen second, I made sure to observe and make notes of my surroundings.

As dawn peeked, Kenneth took the car home to tend to our furkids, before returning in time in the early morning. The message was for all Malaysians to march towards the square, where the Bersih coalition would meet everyone. Different points of the march began from around central Kuala Lumpur. My heart began beating a little faster as we left our home. The time is now. *May we be safe*, I say a little prayer in my head.

From my station, together with volunteer lawyers, we emotionally prepped ourselves for the biggest rally ever in Malaysia. Being the more excited one, Kenneth had already prepared a concoction of milk solution that was supposed to reduce the teargas' stinging effect. I had on the yellow Bersih shirt, track pants, a scarf to tie around my nose and goggles to prevent smog. I continued to keep in touch with my girlfriends around town who were also joining the march with their group of friends.

Slowly but surely, the signal was getting jammed. As I was live-blogging the whole event from my phone, I suddenly find the process of uploading my photos in not smooth but throttled speeds. At that moment, I panicked a little. If I can't publish my photos and captions, I'm not going to be able to deliver the news. I looked up, and everyone around me was either showing their phones to the person next to them, or lifting their phones higher up in the sky as if that would enable them to get a better signal.

There were vans nearby with alien-looking trackers, and we all assumed they were signal jammers. I had already gone out with some live posts and pictures, but I guess I had to go offline and just continue updating via Twitter.

By noon, our group became bigger and bigger, and the sky was scorching. News reports started coming in that it looked like 20,000 people had descended upon Kuala Lumpur. It was massive! We waited for instructions to start marching. The barbed wire and special force were staying put. Then we heard it.

It was a faint bell.

Somebody in the crowd said they were getting messages that protesters had already broken through the barbed wire.

'Stay put!' one of the activists spoke through the loudhailer.

The second bell rang.

The special armed forces, with their batons, and red armours started backing away.

'Wait, a minute, I think . . .' my voice trailed away as a large truck approached. We all knew what it was immediately. Either they were going to smoke us home, or they were going to shoot pellets at us.

Suddenly, from both ends, the barb wire broke.

The third bell rang, and the truck sprayed a huge cloud of smoke at us! At first, the smoke came at us like small ripples of waves. Then, thick plumes of smoke came billowing at us like an angry dragon just breathed its fire.

The smell, oh the smell. I couldn't describe it, to begin with. I would say the gas smelled somewhat 'acidic-vinegar'. And if you're not wearing protective goggles, the pain grips you intensely that you might even think you're going blind.

It's not something you will forget easily for the rest of your life.

Everyone ran topsy-turvy for cover, into small lanes, out to the bigger roads. I ran behind Kenneth, as he started filming the commotion with my DSLR. The chemicals started to get more and more intense, as the fumes that hit the ground and nearby buildings enveloped all of us in a cloud of vapours.

I held tightly onto Kenneth's backpack as he started to move forward and forward progressively.

'Back off, back off, *nowwwww*! It's too strong!' I tugged his bag.

He didn't hear me, and I could see from the footage he was shooting that we already had a winner. But, I let go and ran along with the other protesters.

A smoke can flew near me, and landed just a few steps after me. I looked at another protester, a young Malay boy who was coughing and covering his mouth with a black scarf, and he yelled at me, 'Kick it back!'

I tried, but I missed it, and he managed to take a full swing at it.

I continued to run alongside the other protesters. When you're running really fast in a group, I'm not sure if you ever experienced this, but there's this 'runner's high' and you feel like you've been hit by a rush of adrenaline. My initial reaction was to not get caught. And my second reaction was to get out of harm's way as the chemicals in the tear gas was starting to leave an intense pain in my chest.

When we felt like we were out of danger's sight, I stopped at a pavement and watched everyone helping one another. A shopkeeper left a bucket of water for people to wash their eyes. Another was dousing a young man's face with a milky solution from his bottle. The scene was chaotic, yet there was something poetic about people coming together, helping one another. This is the Malaysia I know and grew up to love.

After dousing my face with the milky concoction I carried in my bag, the intense pain soon subsided. That chest pain I had earlier on, the one I thought I was going to die from, soon became a thing of the past.

My vision slowly came back to me, and my eyes weren't stinging anymore.

Somehow, Kenneth and I reunited near Central Market, an iconic touristy marketplace selling arts and traditional crafts. There were fewer people on the roads now, and seeing I'm no longer walking alone, I gained the courage to stay on and to continue with the live reporting.

We decided to make our way to Jalan Pudu, to assess the situation there. We crossed over and walked up the pedestrian bridge overlooking the main bus terminal on Jalan Pudu. He took a few more shots of the crowd, while I continued updating live news.

'Bersih! Bersih! Bersih!' the crowd was chanting 'clean' thrice. The remaining braver activists had stayed on as their confidence bolstered with each chant resonating through the buildings. Seeing their smiling faces, it calmed me and I decided to stay on for a few more hours.

It started to rain cats and dogs, so it was a good thing we took refuge under the bridge and took out our raincoats.

We walked down the bridge to join the marching crowd. And that's when we got hit unexpectedly again. A few more trucks were approaching the main road. I walked nearer to one of it and presented myself as a member of the press. A cop ignored me, while the other told me to stand closer to the group. Upon inspection, I noticed a policeman pouring chemicals into the truck, and you could very well see clearly the danger sign on the bottle. I snapped a few photos. Then I left the cop's side and joined the crowd.

When I got back to the street, Kenneth was chatting to another protester, and they were exchanging some gleeful hand motions. Next thing you know, four to five plainclothesmen pounced on the guy. The protester did not resist the arrest at all, and he brought both of his hands up to show he was unarmed. After the initial confusion wore away, my feelings turned to shock, and then anger. The other surrounding protesters then started to crowd the plainclothesmen and the situation looked dire.

The man continued to remain calm even though the rest of us were caught in a roiling mess of shock, anger, fear and hesitation. He had both of his arms cuffed with two zip ties and his body pushed to the ground.

Kenneth jumped in to stop them, and I screamed at the group to break it off. It was fucking ridiculous. First of all, the man was clearly unarmed. Secondly, four of them shoved his face towards the tar road, which was unnecessary! I continued snapping photos on my Nikon, to which one of them turned to me, pushed my camera and shouted at me to stop photographing.

I tried to stay calm but I was clearly fuming. He was already threatening physical harm by doing so, and I had every right to photograph the whole commotion. I shouted back in Bahasa, 'Kenapa tak boleh?' but my screams fell on deaf ears.

Best thing of all? All those photographs were useful when I got to use them in a civil court, which I will dissect later.

After the cops lugged him away, my heart sank. There was nothing I could do at that point but hope the Bar Council lawyers would assist him.

We continued walking on Jalan Pudu. It was probably late evening, and helicopters were still swirling above us. It felt like most of the crowd had dispersed, but a few thousand had yet remained in the heart of the city.

'Ting, ting, ting!'

'What the f . . . ' I mouthed as a few trucks came hosing all of us down with a water cannon. We ran as fast as we could, and you could see some of the protesters running into Tung Shin hospital to take refuge from the stinging chemical waters. That's when I witnessed it all; we would have read newspaper headlines a few days later that the Inspector General Police denied water cannon being fired into the hospital's vicinity.

Blasphemy! Lies!

There were footages uploaded to YouTube of the incident which clearly showed the stupidity.

Everyone ran towards the end of Jalan Pudu, and that's when we decided to cut it short and head home. The size of the group had tapered down and there were less actions on the roads now. Kenneth and I didn't speak to one another on our journey home; we were still reeling from the many effects of the rally: the burning feeling left in our throats and chest, the muscle tensions in our bodies and the shock of seeing a protester getting caught before our eyes. We simply understood the scale of this event, and we needed our own time to process it.

As we walked towards home, a neighbour who was getting into his car saw us and flashed us a thumbs up. We nodded and gave him our tired smiles.

After a cold shower, with burnt eyes and skin, I continued working from home, sifting through all the hundreds of images and videos I took with my camera and phone. Kenneth quietly worked at his table, and I, at mine, as we pulled together our narratives: a blow-by-blow timeline of happenings. Once a while, I would pop over and ask for a specific video scene, and he would look like he was singularly focussed on his task.

Even though I went to bed a little after 2 a.m. that day, it took a while to quiet down the busy thoughts that were still running through my mind.

By the next day, right before noon, all the chosen photos and videos were up on the news homepage I was working on. Seeing my name in the photo credits, a sense of accomplishment washed over me. It was the best feeling ever, and I had this powerful, Intuitive feeling I would be experiencing something bigger to come. I couldn't explain it; I just knew it by heart.

The result of the coverage garnered millions of page views. Video views doubled each day. I was still in a daze from the event of magnified proportions. My first street protest—both from the perspectives of a reporter and an activist—which I'd remember for a long time.

The next few days proved to be tumultuous as newspapers reported police violence and brutality. Opposition leader Anwar was injured, Bersih chief Ambiga alongside Islamic party PAS president Abdul Hadi Awang and Batu MP Tian Chua had been arrested.

Soon after, the Human Rights Commission of Malaysia (Suhakam) called for a public inquiry to compile reports from witnesses at the Bersih rally. It was slated to be on 12 October 2011.

Kenneth was adamant he speaks out, and whilst I had some footage to share, I decided it was my civic duty to give my testimonial as well. After giving our names, we were told that a total of thirty-six witnesses had been identified, and about four to five witnesses will be issued with a subpoena. I didn't know that the police had also agreed to cooperate, so basically, I might have just put up my identity to let the whole of Malaysia know.

Chaired by Commissioner Prof Datuk Dr Khaw Lake Tee, I was the third witness to be called to the stand after the first witness, a member of the Bar Council, who testified that tear gas was fired at generally peaceful protesters; and second witness Kenneth, who told the inquiry that he saw police firing water cannons into Tung Shin hospital.

In my enquiry I brought up three important photos from my footage: the first being a cop who left his rifle on the road as he rubbed his eyes, clearly stained from the teargas vapours, and I asked the inquiry if what he did was safe, and would he had harmed people for leaving his weapon unattended? The second photo was a cop pouring toxic chemicals into the truck, and I had the danger sign zoomed-in very clearly. The third series of images were of the protester, who four plainclothes policemen ambushed, violently pushed to the road, and I asked if it was necessary to be manhandled by so many?

A rep from the Polis Diraja Malaysia (PDRM) stood up to ask me, *who'd I work for*. Now, the court stayed silent as I gathered my thoughts surrounding the question. What a pompous way of directing it to me! Who does he think he is?

So I said the first name that came to my mind: Bill Gates.

At that moment, I could see heads turned and facing one another at the audience gallery. Oops, can't retract that now. But it would be funny to imagine the inspector go a Google Search and go, 'Uhm?'

He started scribbling in his notes, and I continued to wait for the next question, but that was all. So I took my seat back at the gallery with a blasé expression.

After the inquiry ended, hordes of fellow reporters came up to us to get our sound bites, and I didn't comment much safe for fact-checking my name. It was a nerve-racking experience, to say the least. The cameras' flashes were going, recorders were almost up to your nose and I reminded myself that I am a journalist as well, and the reporters were also doing their job. But to be interviewed and put on a spotlight like that; I didn't expect it at all and it was exhausting going through the motions twice.

By the next day, the news was splashed across all the leading daily newspapers, with reports published in Indonesia and Singapore. There was a tiny mugshot of me as well, and I was praying so hard my mum didn't see the news. See, I had quite a sheltered upbringing and if I was naughty or up to no good, mum would always throw the cops will arrest you statement in order to put a stop to my nonsensical behaviour then. The older generation like hers, have always abode the law, kept their heads down and grown parochial.

I guess I didn't weigh the consequences of the inquiry because the next thing I know, I got a phone call from mum, who was screaming at me.

'I can't believe you just spoke out against the government! Do you know they will come after us? They will come after me?'

It always begins with a 'they', like, who 'they' would be? And also, the fear-mongering nonsense.

'I'm going to publish in the newspaper that I am disowning you!'

'Erm okay, ma, whatever. I don't see how this is helping anything, and I don't know why you have to be so scared,' I replied nonchalantly.

She slammed the phone down on me. I started to get worried. A sudden thought crossed my mind, *what if she was right?* Would *they* go after my family and threaten them with scare tactics? I'm now no longer a journalist, but a journalist who spoke about police brutality on a stand. The last thing I'd want for myself and for my family is to suddenly . . . *disappear.*

My aunties texted to give moral support. They said I did the right thing. But did I? I was just an unknown low-key citizen slash writer who's just doing her job. And now, it seems I'm getting flack for doing what I think was right. Even as the weeks passed, Kenneth and I got stares at public spots; one time at a restaurant where a family group was hushing and staring at us, then pointing. I thought I had tucked my shirt into my underpants or something.

There is no anonymity when you choose to do something bigger than yourself. And I made that decision on my own to speak out.

***

One morning, like every other morning when Kenneth walks me and my beagle to work, it happened that he needed to buy smokes. So I told him to hurry as I held onto Qyno's leash just below my office, on a grassy patch, in case my dog needed to pee.

I looked across to the entrance of my office, and strangely saw a man lurking about. And you could tell from his behaviour that he was waiting for somebody. Dressed in plain shirt, pants, but with shiny black shoes, I immediately knew he was 'one of the men in black', probably the special force set up after the Bersih public inquiry.

The man noticed I was staring at him, and he immediately, I kid you not, started to 'film' me with a small handheld camera in his left hand. My heart started to pound. Half of me wanted to walk over with Qyno to question him, but the other half of me froze. I didn't want to make a scene, but I could, after all, there was a police beat behind me, and I could jolly well scream that a man was HARASSING me, and maybe the cops would jump on him, and the stranger would have to identify himself to be, TAHDAH, a cop, himself!

But I didn't. I just stood there and stared at him, as he continued filming me, and he walked past me, the nerve. I made a few steps towards him just enough to quickly heed off, and Kenneth appeared only in time.

I pointed at the previous space where he last stood at and told Kenneth the 'special op' man was filming me in broad daylight. It felt like he was trying to intimidate me, but I decided to stand my ground and be assertive by winning the staring game.

Kenneth quickly texted his friends, asking for advice, and I was told to jot down the exact details of this situation: the where, when, who and how.

That was the first and last intimidation that happened to me. I didn't see nor felt anyone following me after.

Two years after that rally, the country was prepping for its elections. I was in touch with one of my contacts; he worked alongside de facto opposition leader Anwar Ibrahim. I saw it as a chance to secure an exclusive interview with the prominent politician. And as nervous as I am about speaking to one of the well-known and outspoken leaders, I had to make a choice—to be sure, I roped in my other editor as he worked for The Star, and had lots of experience under his belt. We couldn't confirm the interview date, but all we knew was to be on standby so that it could happen on the day itself that I had requested through my contact.

'Eh, my boss can do the interview,' my contact tells me over my phone.

'Oh, my God! Ok cool! I'll be conducting the interview on the phone with my editor since we can't meet him. When, yeah?'

The contact then dropped the bomb; Anwar was only free in the next hour. So in true panic fashion, I jumped at the opportunity and said yes! Trouble was, I only had one hour to prep the interview questions, so I hustled my news editor who was managing the website's app to sit in with me and put two brains together.

That phone interview with Anwar—what can I say, we had a few missed moments—I wished I'd say we had the biggest scoop, but Anwar being the media-savvy person, gave PR-friendly answers, and my editor and I didn't quite grill him the way I'd have liked to. Nevertheless, that triumphant moment of securing an exclusive interview left a lasting mark in our career path as a journalist. When you're going through the motions, every day brings a new set of challenges. The pressures that come with the job is insurmountable. If a door of opportunity is presented before us, we'd find ways to address them, document them and fulfil both of our roles in supporting democracy and the search for truth reporting.

I never return to news reporting after that stint with the online media organization. Life had taken a new turn for me as I had left Malaysia for Singapore for another media role but instead, in lifestyle reporting. I figured this was the best way to leave a legacy behind, your life's work at that time.

Sometimes when I think back of this moment, I didn't think I was so brave at all. But if you ask me, if I'd relive this historic moment all over again, I'd say yes in a heartbeat.

How an Asian Woman Journalist Promotes Diversity

By Valencia Tong

'I set out to discover the why of it, and to transform my pleasure into knowledge,' French poet Charles Baudelaire once said.

And like Baudelaire, I have set out on a journey to transform my passion for art and writing into a serious endeavour through the lens of art journalism for the past decade. Art nourishes the soul and it has been an inseparable part of my life. In our fast-paced modern life, there is a need for people to pause and think about the meaning behind mundane everyday existence. Art provides a platform for people to engage in intellectual dialogues to connect with one another. Journalism magnifies such impact by circulating content to reach readers worldwide. From New York's Chelsea to London's Mayfair, and from Singapore's Gillman Barracks to Hong Kong's Central, I have travelled to the world's top art markets to celebrate the latest developments of the cultural sector.

The difference between Baudelaire and I, however, is that he saw the world through the gaze of a flaneur—a role that was typically associated with privileged men of leisure—while I capture my experiences as a female writer of colour. Behind every piece of writing I have published, online and in print, locally and internationally, are words that are left unsaid yet experienced by hundreds of thousands of women worldwide when they travel. Bombarded by questions like 'Where are you from?' and 'Why are you alone?' from friendly faces and strangers alike during my work internationally as a female writer, I have started to wonder whether it is the anomaly for women to have their own sense of agency to go where they want, with or without someone to accompany them. Being told to 'smile,' to 'be polite' or to get a 'chaperone' seems to be the last thing that I need. Ironically, sometimes when I extend my invitation out of generosity, I have been met with responses delivered half-jokingly such as 'Is the art gallery visit a date?' It seems like adventurous solo female travelers are destined to have to explain themselves over and over again. All of the above experiences have made me realize the growing importance of female voices being heard, no matter in everyday interactions, in the workplace, in the art world and in the publishing industry.

In the recent decade, the exponential growth of the Asia-Pacific region, especially the art market in China and South East Asia, has turned financial hubs like Shanghai, Hong Kong and Singapore into major art destinations. The diverse artistic expressions in these regions and the plethora of high-profile VIP events have attracted a wide range of international galleries to set up their Asian outposts. Celebrities and well-heeled art collectors have flocked to art fairs, which have usually been the talk of the town. Covering these events has meant that the glamour portrayed in the glossy sales reports of sold-out exhibitions is only a small fraction of what the general public sees. The perks of being an art writer includes being able to eavesdrop on conversations on VIP preview days, which range from dialogues between art advisors and gallerists to museum curators' occasional incisive remarks on the quality of an artist's work. At charity galas, what is often reported are the price achieved in silent auctions. Not surprisingly, the human elements that are behind the scenes are left out: when celebrities and art world dignitaries grit their teeth until they can no longer hide the fact that their towering six-inch high heels hurt; when art collector couples bicker about whether their latest art acquisitions match their walls; and when guests have had just a little too much champagne. As you can see, the pre-Covid art world thrived on human interactions. What interests me are the micronarratives left out in mainstream media, and more importantly, in traditional newsrooms.

However, the Covid-19 pandemic has changed both journalism and the art scene in drastic ways. Adopting cost-cutting measures such as layoffs and furloughs, traditional newsrooms have begun tightening their focus during the pandemic on key business stories. This has meant that culture and lifestyle content are the first to be reduced or eliminated, as art has typically been seen as 'non-essential'. Meanwhile, in-person art events have scaled down to comply with social distancing measures or have moved online. Numerous cultural events have been postponed and cancelled, no matter whether they are small-scale productions, charity galas or well-funded auctions. As such, there are fewer stories to report on and even fewer news outlets to publish art news. To adapt to the changes brought by the Covid-19 pandemic, I began exploring new ways of tackling the issues by bringing attention to my work through alternative methods online.

Interestingly, this pivotal moment has accelerated the decentralization of journalism, as new forms of journalistic practices have emerged to adapt to the exponential growth of social media. The lockdown in many parts of the world, as well as the work from home arrangement, meant that Internet usage of large populations worldwide has increased. Circulation of images, videos and creative content has never been faster, and whenever people have spare time while being confined in their homes, they search for newsworthy and educational content to 'like' and 'share' on their digital devices. Both news corporations and the art world embrace technology readily, churning out content which appeals to the audience whose limited attention span can largely be explained by the information overload viewers experience. When museums start asking the general public to recreate famous paintings with household items, and when journalists actively embed crowdsourced social media posts into their articles in order to tell this story, it is clear that the Covid-19 pandemic has fostered the development of the bottom-up approach towards communication and storytelling. When my content received numerous 'likes' and 'shares', I felt like I have made an impact. The diversity of voices being elevated through social media, to a certain extent, hints that the top-down way of disseminating information has gradually become obsolete.

In the past, art writers can make or break an artist's career. I, however, am more interested in uplifting those that deserve to be known by a larger audience. Not only do I profile and interview artists, curators, gallerists and collectors from established epicentres of art, I also give voice to emerging art world rising stars in places such as Hong Kong, Japan, Korea, Singapore, Taiwan, Thailand and Indonesia. Having worked with editors based in Asia, America and Europe, I am constantly amazed by the connectivity of the art world as jet setting journalists never stop discovering new cross-cultural content for the global audience worldwide. Globalization has been a blessing for the art world in the recent years, as young professionals and high net worth individuals scour the Internet for trophy works of art to add to their collection. Their curiosity fuels the need for sophisticated art analysis as they strive to educate themselves, to cultivate taste and to make informed decisions. Art writers are at the forefront of the creation of quality content to meet the demands of the elite. Dissecting works of art and interpreting data of the latest trends involve both art and science. However, I would argue that the danger of only writing for trade publications is that this alienates the general public, so I have diversified my work to not only serve the academics and aesthetes, but also comment on popular culture, as well as the intersection of art and other industries such as music, fashion, real estate and technology. This is the beauty of diversity in an art writer's work—every day is different.

To create diversity in the field of art journalism, we must dismantle the notion that only 'straight white males' have the gravitas to shape how people perceive the value of art. We must stop the mindless assumption that the 'opinions' of 'straight white males' carry more weight. We must think critically and question the authority of the experts and gatekeepers who select what gets included. More importantly, we must learn to read between the lines. What people tend to forget is that the relationship between reading and writing is inseparable. Literacy, to a large extent, is not only about the technical aspect of basic building blocks like grammar and vocabulary. Literacy is also about listening to what is being said and contemplating whether the status quo makes sense. Literacy is the foundation that empowers people to recognize and celebrate differences.

Nurturing loyal readers is the key to cultivating diversity in our world at large, and I have cultivated a loyal following for my work.

In order for high-quality writing to be read, and for diverse voices to be heard, there needs to be enough readers who do not compromise on quality. It is ultimately a question of demand and supply; when there are readers who, with their clicks and subscriptions, show the owners of media outlets that there is a demand for content that showcase diverse voices, there is more incentive to publish these stories. With the bottom line becoming more relevant to the pandemic-hit publishing industry, SEO analytics that reflect customer demand are now more important than ever in the era of falling advertising revenue. As my world of work undergoes rapid transformation, I believe that digital literacy will matter more than ever in my future. The power is in the hands of the readers, whose participation contribute to the number of page views of the content of their choice, which in turn determine what is popular and gets seen and heard.

Equally important is to nurture prolific writers, who channel the power of the pen to craft educational content to stimulate dialogue surrounding the topic of diversity. It is no surprise that in order to be a good writer one must read voraciously. The problem, is that today, in our world proliferated by smartphones and digital devices, people no longer have patience to read. Long-form content is reduced as it is deemed too tedious to read. It has become increasingly difficult to vet content for their quality because fact-checking has become lax when social media is the preferred place for people to read news. Since I read a wide range of texts to enrich my knowledge and improve my writing skill, I intend to lead by example by empowering others to do the same. This is why it is both a privilege and a responsibility for journalists to be role models for aspiring writers, and to insist on quality.

I find art journalism a wonderful niche to strike a balance between satisfying the need of the readers for large eye-catching images and creating intellectually stimulating content. An article about art is more accessible for the general public than a complex social commentary. It is neither frowned upon to only look at images in an article about art to understand what is happening, nor is it inappropriate to jump straight to the text to read the whole story. Art journalism engages the mind and the eyes; it guides the readers what to look, where to look and how to look. I believe that art journalism is didactic yet not boring at all. However, it would be arrogant to say that journalists are the ones who educate the public, and the readers are ones who passively absorb information. Newspaper columns exist to provide a platform for dialogue, and it is always humbling to engage with people from all walks of life who view the same work of art through different angles. With the rise of social media, it is easier to start conversations about artworks and talk about diversity in the art world with readers worldwide.

Tensions between populist and elitist writing have always existed throughout the history of art journalism. How does an art journalist pique the interest of the general public on rare, exclusive art events in the notoriously opaque art market? Likewise, how does an art journalist make art world academics and art collectors, who often live in a bubble, feel interested in sharing their expertise and their collections to the public? It is up to art journalists to search for opportunities in every nook and cranny to tell stories which champion diversity through mass media. The ability to speak the language with people from vastly different social and cultural backgrounds, and to synthesize ideas into words that touch hundreds of thousands of lives, is an asset that art journalists possess.

The power of community should not be underestimated. Just because international travel is almost impossible during the pandemic, coupled with the dwindling number of cultural events, it does not mean that art journalism is dead. Just because we are advised to stay at home during the pandemic, it does not mean that the domestic sphere is where female journalists have to feel where they belong. Just because art has been deemed 'non-essential' does not mean that the voices of those I elevate are 'non-essential'. This is why my extensive professional affiliations in multiple sectors have been important channels for me to reach out to new people no matter their background. Thanks to technology, the division between private and public has become increasingly irrelevant, and both the art world and the journalism sector have been quick to innovate to find ways to break down barriers for the dissemination of information.

One aspect that the pandemic has highlighted is the urgent need for universal access to the Internet to bring about diversity and inclusion.

With everything moving online, from e-learning to digital news, it is time to think about how people who are traditionally not the target audience of art journalists can benefit from having access to content through the Internet. Schoolchildren, the elderly and people with a disability now have more time to explore cultural content now that they have more free time at home. For them to feel connected, art plays an important role in helping them appreciate the beauty of being alive in this world. Amidst the pandemic, art writers can do more to play an active role in using their expertise to help foster art appreciation in the general public, making art accessible for not only commercial purposes, but also to provide a sense of optimism. It is the perfect time to practice gratitude—for being alive, for having stable Internet, and for slowing down to rethink the possibilities of a post-Covid world.

As I reflect upon my journey as a female art writer, I have begun to redefine my role as not just capturing the truth of what is happening in the art world, but also tell stories that are often left untold for people who have never thought of being part of this dialogue. Perhaps, what I am doing now is more than a flâneur. Not satisfied with just being a fly on the wall—a distant observer—I have been transforming the Covid crisis into an opportunity for connectivity and diversity. Armed with a pen, a notepad and a laptop computer, I may not be able to travel the world temporarily, but my mind is freer than ever right now to think out of the box. As a female art writer of colour, I can confidently say that I have not only set out to discover the 'why' of what's happening in the world at large nowadays, I have also explored the 'how' of creating diversity. I am proud to have transformed my pleasure into knowledge, and more importantly, transformed my knowledge into the pleasure of instilling in my readers the love for art and writing. Since words transcend time and space, I hope to leave a legacy that history never forgets.

Welcome to Journalism, Welcome to Malaysia

By Ista Kyra

'GET OUT!'
'GET LOST!'
'GO AWAY!'

From my days as a rookie reporter to a little bit more seasoned journalist, I heard this phrase too often.

Abuse was a common and constant side effect of the job.

Mostly, I was at the receiving end of varying degrees of verbal intimidation but there were several times where it had transgressed into the realm of criminal harassment.

A constant feature of the job was to be constantly vigilant of potential threats. Be it in the form of open intimidation or the more sinister, 'friendly, neighbourhood' predatory types.

The regularity with which I was being told that I was 'unwanted' at any time or place, simply due to my job, occurred so often that I eventually considered it to be a job requisite.

It made little difference which beat of journalism I was covering, whether it was a bread and butter issue, courts, crime or politics on either side of the divide.

Yet, it was in covering politics for the first time that I experienced a jarring encounter, which would frame my outlook about my country's people and its leaders.

This happened right at the start of my foray into journalism, in which I had the chance to join a prominent news organization with employment attached to the bureau in my hometown, Ipoh.

At the time in 2010, I was a bright-eyed idealist who had felt proud to score the reporting gig after a full year of doing multiple freelance works as a tuition teacher, receptionist and other jobs unrelated to my passion for writing.

The bureau chief then, was the late Husairy Othman, who had hired me as the sole female and youngest member of a team comprising seasoned male reporters and photographers in their late thirties to fifties.

Over the course of several months, Husairy would send me out on several test assignments across different beats, where I had to prove that I was capable of delivering.

When he finally decided I was ready to cover politics, it came in the form of an unexpected call from HQ and a seeming challenge to gauge whether I was truly cut out for the job.

He had relayed the assignment to me in his smoke-filled office room, telling me that I was required to seek out a prominent senior politician and get reactions to some specific questions.

Seated with his back to a large window, where the blinds were perpetually drawn down and pendaflour light remained constantly on, he said, 'I just got off the phone from HQ. They want us to run an exclusive on this guy,' pointing to the image of a veteran opposition lawmaker on one of the pages in a newspaper.

'They want us to get an answer from him, if he had indeed worked for the Singapore prime minister before, as some parties are alleging.'

I stood rooted before him, all ears.

'The good news is, he can be found at this address. Apparently, there's a press conference happening in an hour's time,' Husairy said, texting me the location of the lawmaker's office.

'The bad news is the seniors are busy and we need this story by the end of the day so this will be your first interview with a prominent lawmaker,' Husairy explained.

'You think you can handle this?' he asked with furrowed eyebrows, an expression I had come to imprint as either disdain or disapproval.

Being just a few months shy into the job, I was both nervous and elated at being entrusted with the assignment.

I was not someone who knew much about politics although I was open to exploring the beat. I had only started reading the actual news sections in the paper when I began working as a reporter, before that only the comics and youth pullout interested me. I hardly ever glanced at the headlines under the politics section, finding them to be so far removed from my personal reality.

I could carry a conversation about the different political parties and personalities, solely based on eavesdropping on Kopitiam discussions and that was truly not much to speak of.

Yet, I felt compelled to take up the assignment and do it well to be accepted as a reliable member of my new work team. More than getting my byline printed in the newspapers, I had come to crave the respect and validation from the senior reporters in the office.

Jaspal Singh, Chandra Sagaran, Ikhwan Munir and the late Wong Tuck Keong were seasoned and well-known pressmen who had regaled me with tales of their adventure and mettle in covering various events in Perak.

So despite feeling some misgivings, I nodded my head to Husairy and told him I could definitely handle the assignment.

I stymied the butterflies in my stomach from turning into a full-blown panic attack by focusing on the practical aspects of my task; getting directions and making sure I was on time to cover the press conference.

In those days, it was common for journalists from different publications to be told apart by the colour of their lanyards. This was usually marked with their organization's brand or logo, with a media tag dangling on the other end.

As a still new and unconfirmed addition to the press, I had yet to receive my official media tag. I was given the company's lanyard but I preferred to don one that was more suited to my aesthetic tastes. Now this seemingly frivolous detail, likely played a significant role in the warm welcome I received into the press conference.

There were no bodyguards or people who actually checked the tags. It was commonly presumed that if you turned up at a press conference, you likely had business to be there. Therefore, up until I decided to approach the lawmaker in question to seek the specific answers I was tasked with, I could not have predicted the nonplussed feelings I would end up with at the end.

As it were, the lawmaker's intended statements at the conference had nothing related to the questions my HQ was interested in. When I arrived, there were already journalists occupying all the seats, so I stood at the back but close enough to listen and jot down notes.

From my line of sight, I could see the lawmaker in question without obstruction. I looked directly at him as he spoke, trying to appear like I belonged there and that I knew what I was doing.

The poundings of my racing heart seemed to become more palpable with every passing minute.

I was nervously going through all the possible ways I could accomplish my specific task. Should I speak up during question time or reserve it for after the other reporters had left? If I gave away the angle, it might be a lost chance at an exclusive story.

At that moment in time, I had failed to perceive the loadedness of the question I had been sent to ask. To my mind, there was nothing sinister about a Malaysian member of parliament having been previously employed in Singapore. A stint with the Singaporean prime minister, no less, conveyed to me, good experience to list on a political resume.

In the midst of all my mental calculations, I suddenly realized the press conference had ended and reporters were packing to leave. For a moment, I panicked that the politician I needed to interview had got away but I spotted him from across the room, closing an office door behind him.

I dashed over and found myself knocking on his door.

Immediately the voice of the senior man greeted me, 'Come in'.

I held my breath as I gingerly opened the door to enter, seeing the politician looking regally from his desk, poring over stacks of papers.

'Good afternoon sir,' I said, as politely as I could muster. 'I'm a reporter and I would like to interview you.'

He looked up from the stacks of papers and studied me for a while, looking over his giant spectacles and smiling into a wrinkly grin. His demeanor was kindly, as if indulging a young child.

'Please come in, come and sit.'

His manner put me at ease and I started to feel maybe this wasn't going to be so daunting an interview afterall.

As I took out my notebook and recording device, we managed some small talk before he asked, 'Which media are you from?'

I casually replied with the name of my organization, unsuspecting that this would quickly flip the mood in the room.

Before I could get a chance to ask anything, I noticed his face had turned red and was contorting into an expression of disgust.

'Get out,' he said, behind clenched teeth.

This only confused me and I said, 'I beg your pardon, sir?'

'I said . . . get out! GET OUT!' his voice now raised, he himself stood up over his table.

I stood up as well and tried to explain again that I was a reporter and that I was just here to ask a simple question.

He must have been caught off-guard at my earnestness because he ventured to ask what it is I had come to find out.

The moment I uttered my question, the senior man appeared to be almost frothing at the mouth.

He bellowed again for me to get out as he started pacing behind his desk.

Next thing I know, he was slamming his fist on the desk, and even slapped away a stack of books as he gestured for me to remove myself from the building.

I was completely perplexed and in shock. Why should I have been so unceremoniously thrown out without any valid explanation at all? I found it unbecoming of a senior person and immediately changed my mind about looking up to this personality, whom I knew many in my circle, including my parents, to admire.

When I recounted my experience to Husairy and the seniors at the office, all I got was a hearty round of chuckles. The way they guffawed at my naivete, I suspect they would not have been happier if I had returned with actually having accomplished the task I was set out to do.

When I finally caught up with the thorny history between the news organization I represented and the veteran politician I was sent to cover, I understood that I had essentially been dispatched to a landmine scenario, by the bureau chief at the time.

That incident marks my foray into covering politics in Malaysia, and the worst was yet to come.

* * *

Five years later, I began working for an alternative news portal. This meant that I no longer wrote reports that served the agenda of the ruling political parties in the country, who largely controlled stakes in the mainstream media companies.

As a representative of 'alternative' voices outside the mainstream publications, I was actively prevented from attending official functions and refused entry into press conferences.

Although I was primarily covering news in my home state, Perak, I felt the sting of being the 'pariah' at press events much more so because some of the mainstream reporters I had counted as friends soon began distancing themselves from me.

As an 'outsider' of sanctioned press, police raids and device confiscation was a common reality in the newsroom office. The publication I worked for was constantly under threat of being de-licensed.

Suddenly, it was not just enough worrying about being invaded with these types of interruptions, there was also the threat of being 'in' the news as the subject of reports, instead of the ones reporting them.

As a female reporter covering the Perak state assembly, I became the target of intimidation tactics such as being filmed without my knowledge and singled out to be shamed for the length of my skirt or choice of footwear.

It so happened that when I was six months pregnant, my feet had ballooned overnight and I could not fit into my regular shoes. I chose to still turn up and cover the state assembly being held, in the only slippers that I could fit into.

A group of civil servants attempted to have me thrown out for this and had me reported for 'disrespecting' the August House with my choice of dress. This is despite the fact that I never entered the Dewan Negeri and confined myself to the room reserved for press conferences.

When I wasn't being shunned off, I seemed to be the target of objectification.

In one incident, a minister with a father-figure type persona invited me into his office after a press conference, for a supposed friendly chit-chat.

He reached out to salaam, my hand and I took it without suspecting anything. I gradually became uncomfortable when I realized that the more I attempted to pull my hand back, the closer he pulled me towards himself.

He appeared to be trying to distract me with his conversation as he continued to hold my hand in that uncomfortable handshake. He held on for much longer than I would have permitted.

Eventually, the stress and pressures of coping in an environment where one is constantly being bullied, branded and barred from doing their job, simply got to me.

I was eight months pregnant when the online publication I worked at was effectively shut down and branded a threat to national security by the country's Internet regulatory body, Malaysian Communications and Multimedia Commission (MCMC).

My priorities had shifted now that I was anticipating parenthood and I decided to make a career change, shifting into a corporate role that offered better financial returns and less jail time threats.

My new role as a research analyst involved monitoring social media and creating reports on public sentiments towards different brands, organizations and public figures. It seemed like, as much as I wanted to run away from politics, it was still following me around.

I began witnessing divisive behaviours in thousands of social media posts and comments. The tendency to discriminate based on political, religious and racial lines was exaggeratedly amplified on social media platforms.

It was something that, without my prior journalistic experience, where I've had the chance to mingle with a diverse set of people face to face; would easily plunge me into a deep depression about the state of my country and its people.

Ultimately, although I had become used to Malaysians attempting to repel me in various ways and at the receiving end of some extremely rude behaviours as a reporter, I was also privileged to experience the nicest, warm and inspiring hospitality by none other than Malaysians too.

Ironically, these positive, feel-good memories did not take place when I was shoulder to shoulder with the who's who of the country, but in the company of ordinary, humble citizens.

As a woman of mixed Indian-Chinese heritage and being married to a Punjabi, I am all too familiar with being right there in the happy yet occasionally tension-filled, roiling mix of cultural tensions and conflicts.

My very identity has if anything, increased my sensitivity towards these sorts of divisions even as I myself hold different cultures within one person.

I am welcomed yet not completely embraced into either of my family groups, because I am always perceived as belonging to the 'other' ethnicity.

These narratives also play out very much in the politics of the country, national headlines and as a result, social media too.

In Malaysia, what is often published and sensationalized is the extreme polarity between the majority Malay and non-Malay minorities, divided based on race, religion and culture.

Resentment is a significant sentiment between the groups, each feeling as if they received the shorter end of the stick under government policy or economic advantage.

Being called *pendatang* or 'migrant' is an infamous sore point among those in the non-Malay minority, a label that clearly implies unwelcome by the majority Malay community despite having forged years and decades together under one nation.

Being a non-Malay with the privilege of having lived in a Malay kampung for some time, I know that such rude labels are actually antithesis to the heart of Malay traditions or *adat resam* that uphold polite speech and behaviour, especially towards strangers.

The actions and speech of a Malay person are usually guarded as it is often viewed as a marker of one's upbringing. To display ill actions, is to dishonour one's family. Even praise and criticism are often cloaked in imagery and never direct, as can be observed from Malay *peribahasa* or proverbs.

As a journalist, I've also observed how these subtle cues of culture that are seemingly nondescript speak volumes in the art of 'welcome', 'politeness' and 'community'.

I was once deployed to cover an incident involving the abduction and sexual assault of an 11-year-old girl, who had been kidnapped from the streets of her housing neighbourhood while walking to her religious class and then dumped by the roadside somewhere in Gopeng.

Being expected to get an interview with either the victim or the victim's family was a daunting task for me, as I did not feel comfortable asking probing questions to them after their ordeal. I imagined they would not welcome reporters either and likely send us off with expletives, which I would not have faulted them for. Yet, my editors expected me to try and get the story to avoid being 'scooped' by rival press.

After arriving at the victim's neighbourhood and identifying their house, I noticed there were already journalists there, taking leave from the house after graciously thanking them. I saw that one of the journalists was putting on his socks and shoes, which meant they had been allowed entry into the home and perhaps gained access to personal interviews.

My Malay colleague, Abang Shaka, who was with me at the time, called out 'Assalamualaikum' to the family, the Muslim greeting that warranted a reply from another fellow Muslim. They replied and heard our request for interviews but politely declined.

Our hearts sank at this, as we deduced that the journalists we had seen leaving the family's premises earlier may have succeeded in obtaining the interviews.

I scoured the papers the next day to see how the other press may have covered the story but found none of them to have revealed any more insider facts than the ones according to police records.

In discussing this with my Malay colleague, Ros Dalilah, she tells me that this type of behaviour is not new nor alien among the Malay community. According to Ros, this is a classic example of the *budi bahasa* or 'discretion' in Malay culture.

It amazed me that despite having experienced such a violent personal trauma, the victim's family had the grace to remain calm and collected towards prying strangers in the form of journalists.

At a time when they were most vulnerable, having to deal with a traumatic event that befell a young member of their home, this family still possessed the composure to not only speak politely, but also invite reporters into their home and offer refreshments, even as their intention was not to release any public statements.

In my experience, few of our ministers and leaders in public office have shown such poise or maturity towards reporters, even as their positions warrant fielding questions from the press.

Another time, a young mother in Bemban, Batu Gajah, had lost her baby while breastfeeding the child in their home. When reporters arrived, the afflicted family were already holding a *tahlil* ceremony, a Muslim funerary prayer.

In this incident, our group of reporters managed to get invited into the home and were served food and drink while waiting to be granted interviews.

Based on the warm reception, I had assumed that we would be getting an interesting human interest story. Instead, after laying down the tray of glasses with air sirap, the man who kindly served us, informed us that the family did not wish to give any press interviews.

In this strange anomaly, one of my colleagues tried to prolong the conversation, in hopes that the man would soften and relent with some personal story but it didn't pan out that way. In a kind but firm tone, we were told that the family's decision not to release press comments were final.

I later learnt that my Malay colleagues habitually respected the decisions of families not to sensationalize certain details in the news to prevent further *aib* or shame to the afflicted parties.

Another Malay colleague, Norhayati Ablah, informed me that the concept of *menjaga aib* is steeped in the Malay and Muslim traditions and similar to the 'save face' culture of the Chinese.

Over the course of my six-year stint in journalism, where I was surrounded by many ordinary Malaysians of various backgrounds, I have observed them adhering to these common values without pomp or splendour.

These are the kind of stories that never quite make headlines but are no less compelling and important to be told. On the news, in social media and even Parliament debates, the wise ways of the small Malay village are not always at the forefront.

Perhaps, some deem such budi bahasa as no longer relevant, too *kampung* or parochial for modern times, but I personally hold these to be important cornerstones that could uplift our melting pot of a society and rekindle more meaningful exchange that could transcend the divisive rhetorics prevalent today.

I no longer wear the lanyard with reporter credentials, yet, far from regretting my decision to serve in the fourth estate, those years between 2010 and 2016, are among the ones that fill me with a sense of pride and earned wisdom. Memories and learnings from that period now serve as valuable insights that help me to see the underlying context and better frame the issues we continue to face today.

Of Grit and Glamour

By Susanah Cheok

When one's private real life meets her public media life, it can taste somewhat like fries dipped in dark chocolate—incongruent but delicious and more-ish.

The irony is that when what you do for a living is a conversation starter, you tend to not want to talk about it. Somewhat like what is said about comedians—that off-stage, they can be people of few words, who don't like to tell jokes, and the perpetuating myth that clowns are sad.

The fact that it's a conversation starter means that what I used to do to earn my keep was interesting, exciting even, not something many people may hear about every day. Depending on my mood and energy level, I am sometimes happy to regale them with the crazy highs that came with the job—front-row seats at the most coveted shows during fashion week, champagne and fine dining ad nauseum, seeing the world in the name of work, rubbing shoulders with the glitterati, just to name a few things; as well as the stressful low-downs—impossible deadlines, working overnight to meet them, keeping the peace with unhappy clients, and putting on my game face even when assailed by said unhappy clients and impossible deadlines.

This life of extremes was also thankfully hinged together by what I call the grounded normalcy of a quiet, mundane private life—catching up on leisure reading during commutes by cab or MRT; changing out of high heels and flip-flopping to the hawker stall for street-style fare to take away or eat alone; holing up in my modest flat in the suburbs; enjoying the mindless pleasure of retail therapy in anonymity.

And feeling completely happy about it, because I wasn't required to work a room nor make conversation with anyone. Editing a well-known magazine may have its perks, but being an off-duty editor certainly has its privileges too.

If you've ever lived a double-life, you will know what I mean. It's a little bit like being Superman and Clark Kent. You push yourself to perform and embrace the glamour, the glitz, like a dressage show horse, and then, after work hours, you look forward to immersing yourself in the bliss of blending in, to being an ordinary, inconspicuous stable horse. You start to enjoy both sides of your double life and blessedly, the two lives also start to balance each other out. It's a good trade-off.

It takes energy and commitment to consume glamour at the pace I did as the editor-in-chief of a leading magazine. People laugh and say that's hardly work at all. But the inside story from this horse's mouth is that it's damn hard work. But great work nevertheless, if you can get it, because you really grow from it on a personal level, and your world grows too; it becomes expansive and so rich in the sort of experiences and exposure money can't buy.

I remember my first fashion press trip to Paris as a twenty-something. How, when I saw the Eiffel Tower, I wept. The taste of my first authentic French breakfast of croissant and café au lait, and sitting by the window of the typically quaint hotel room I was put up in, watching the world go by from that vantage point, taking in the noise from the bistro right across, watching people clop-clopping by on the cobblestone walkway. I fell so hard for Paris, it crossed my mind to find work as a waitress and live there. It may have been a sorely impractical idea, as I didn't speak more than a smattering of basic French, but to have been given a glimpse of a life beyond what I had back home was to me, a gift in fresh perspective in itself. It let me know there was more than one way to live the life I wanted.

Whilst I was day-dreaming of a life waiting on tables in the city of lights and love, lapping up every charming attraction Paris had to offer, the food, the museums, the cafes, the cathedrals, the impossibly chic people and the complicated but comprehensive metro system, my real task then was to report on two important fashion shows: Dior Couture, which was an intimate, plush affair, with the runway models walking so close to where I sat, I could touch the hems of their skirts, and Kenzo Ready-to-Wear, which was rock-concert spectacular, it made me feel very small, lost, but that was the wonder of it all.

As my career path unfolded, Paris became a sort-of second home. For a good part of the twenty-seven years I spent in the fashion media business, I was travelling to the fabled French city at least twice a year, to attend fashion shows, report on beauty launches and interview fashion's top creative minds. I grew fond of Paris, and after each visit, I felt more comfortable in its environs. There came a time when, with a metro guide in hand, I could find my way to any part of the grand old city. Funnily enough, I can't even manage that in my own tiny island city of Singapore. During each trip to Paris, I would make it a point to explore a new district. Paris brought out the adventuress in me, like a friend whom I saw infrequently, but whom I always looked forward to catching up with and getting to know even better each time.

It is true that the best way to see the fashion collections is at its source, when they are first rolled out to the whole world at the fashion week runways—in Paris, Milan, London, New York, and some might say, Tokyo. That's when you'll not only see the models of the moment in the flesh, but the up-and-coming ingenues. They are otherworldly, with a litheness and bone structure that's ethereal. Hard to imagine, as these seraphim-like creatures glide, stride, clomp, stomp, depending on the mood of the collection and the music, that like us, they also eat, sleep and take bio breaks.

At the shows, when the lights dim, and the first model strides out, when the as-yet-unheard-of music plays, usually some minted dance track, you feel like you've been transported to another universe.

The fashion media life is an education in itself. How can it not be when you are the conduit between the trendsetters and the very people they want to convince to buy into the trends? The insights you are privy to, because it's your job to know: why a designer chooses a certain theme for his or her collection; how a rocket scientist turned the tragedy of a chemical burn into a miracle broth that became one of the world's most famous anti-ageing creams; the secret ingredient in a world-famous chef's addictive whipped potato; and how celebrities are really not so different from us—that they get homesick and yearn for home cooked meals too.

Years ago, I visited the Max Huber research laboratory in Melville, New York, where the famous Crème de la Mer moisturizing cream is made. Among other things, the inside scoop I picked up is that before each batch of formulation is ready, it is first engaged with a certain kind of music, like a sound bath, in order to allow the formulation to produce the right enzymes and cultures. The cream is 'alive' and it can 'hear'. How eye-opening! It takes a card-carrying magazine editor to get to the heart of this, and then share it with the world.

I met Beyoncé in New York when she was the face of True Star, a fragrance endorsed by American fashion designer Tommy Hilfiger. Beyoncé looked even more beautiful than in pictures and film, and very tall. Up close, I saw how radiant she was. She glowed. She was at ease, relaxed, warm and friendly. That was quite a while ago, in 2004, and I don't recall what she said about the perfume anymore, but I remember her talking about missing Houston, from where she hails, and her mum's southern fried chicken.

It's the little unexpected things that stick in the memory. Like how Rihanna was so girlish and giggly at one of our teen magazine cover shoots. How easy-going she was. Like how the late JFK Junior prefers to cycle through the streets of New York than to be chauffeured.

Then again, big events like dinner with the Lauders—Leonard, Evelyn, Aerin and Jane, to be exact, of Estee Lauder Inc—are hard to forget too. With a small group of editors from Singapore, I was invited to their NYC Park Avenue family home one Fall in 2001. It still sounds unreal and dream-like to talk about how we sat around their dining table and feasted on a meal made from the beauty conglomerate's founder, Estee Lauder's favourite family recipes, one of which was a comforting chicken soup dish. I was seated between make-up mogul Bobbi Brown and her husband, Steven Plofker, both of whom I found down-to-earth and genuinely lovely to talk to. Post-dinner, we gathered in the Lauders' living room to pore over family albums, while talking about Christmas plans. I believe I wasn't the only journalist present, who felt positively cocooned in the kindness and warmth of our hosts.

Another 'home visit' of surreal note was to the decadent apartment of Coco Chanel in Rue Cambon, Paris, which is decorated with her treasured artefacts, the most famous and precious of which are her favourite Coromandel screens. Madame Chanel was known to have thirty-two of these foldable panels, which she used to decorate her walls like so much paper, and to give structure to her private space.

As a channel to the stars, I was also inevitably a mini, minor celebrity, and for reasons of being a purveyor of the trendy fashion and beauty lifestyle to our readers, also known as the people the brands and celebrities wanted to reach, I was treated like one too. The premise that you have to try it to know it meant I was inundated with all manner of beauty products—skincare, make-up, haircare, bodycare, facial and spa treatments, you name it.

Fashion brands are much more restrained, but they still find creative ways to let you experience what their brands and products stand for, how they want their brands and products to make our readers, their potential customers, feel—desire, that is, for the latest must-have shoes, apparel and *it* bags.

To most people outside the fashion media industry, this doesn't sound much like work at all, until you realize that so much of the preliminaries need to come into play even before an editor starts engaging with clients, designers, and interview subjects. Taking it all in, deconstructing the message, the look, the idea, the concept, the real deal of the celebrity, whether designer, musician, or actress, also means stripping away the pomp and pageantry of the launch, so that you can get to the heart of what you want to tell your readers. But then sometimes the pomp and pageantry *are* the very news points you want to share. It's the delicate sifting work of editing, spotting the gems, knowing what to keep, like panning for gold.

That's just the one glitzy layer of it. The pretty veneer that those outside the industry see. It's called the punishing publishing grind for a reason. I like to compare creative production work to running on a treadmill, because by hook or by crook, the magazine must come out, get published, hit the newsstands, non-stop, month after month. After the courtship and the lovemaking come the birth pangs, which are sometimes so painful, you tell yourself, 'never again!', until and the 'baby' comes out and the afterglow, post-birth, makes the pain a distant memory and you can't wait to get back out there to do it all over again.

I see the monthly production grind of magazine publishing as experiences and conversations becoming true stories and snapshots of realism, albeit with some escapist digital enhancement, but not too much, and then through a process of pagination, all these become a book that sends a new and exciting message out for that month.

It takes thought, time, people and their creative skills, definitely dexterity and eagle-eye sharps, especially when proofreading. I've had many surreal memories of proofreading layouts late into the night, dressed to the ninths from a ball, because publishing deadlines are immovable. That's when the show horse becomes a work horse.

One of the deepest satisfactions I derived from this demanding yet sometimes seemingly frivolous job, was being heard. There is nothing quite as empowering as communicating your say, and in the process, shape the consciousness of your readers too. There is nothing quite as positive and fulfilling as being in the business of informing women on how to be the best that they can be.

This very public life of high-octane glitz and glamour can be a pressure cooker, especially when the merciless screws of production deadlines are tightened. And they say fashion is unforgiving. That's when I truly appreciate the escape into obscurity, of not being known and not socializing. To eat, not a degustation meal, but something simple, like a bowl of noodles from the corner food stall, to shop where I don't need to dress the part, to dine alone, with only a good book for company. I was grateful for the balance that being inscrutable and being off the merry-go-round brought to that sometimes too-manic work life.

The word surreal is defined as having the qualities of surrealism, something bizarre, for example, 'a surreal mix of fact and fantasy'; weird, strange, unearthly. For me, some days were all of the above, so yes, here's the long introduction to my former surreal double life as a fashion magazine editor.

No other work helps you to grow the nerve to work a room as effectively, nor to make conversation with anyone—from the movers and shakers of this world to the mum-next-door—so naturally. To engage like you belong in the world of celebrities, to develop a discerning eye and taste buds, and yet be disciplined enough to turn up at the office armed and ready for the creative rigors, and then be grounded enough to return home, happy with your real life, because it is that which also recharges you.

To this day, it amazes me how I managed to get my foot in and I'm still wondering what I did to deserve this sort of work falling onto my lap. When I first started out, this was my idea of being a writer—me at a corner desk, cranking out stories, to inform and entertain, hoping to make someone's day, one article at a time, until I reached the age of retirement. In my naivete, I did not foresee the glamour nor the grit. I guess the publishing universe had other plans.

In July 2016, my earlier modest dream did finally come true. I left corporate publishing and became a freelance writer and editor, one who's ironically churning out stories from a corner desk in my living room, thankful for the chance to still make a difference, one small article at a time.

From Beverly Hills
to Battambang

By Ann Marie Chandy

When I checked in at the Viceroy L'ermitage Beverly Hills in 2003, I nearly keeled over. I had never seen anything like it; calling it extravagant would be an understatement. My room was ever-so-luxurious, with custom-designed furniture, elegant fabrics and a bathroom that seemed the size of a small apartment! It was all a little too much for this small-town girl who grew up in the sleepy-hollow of Malacca, Malaysia.

Thanks to my job as a lifestyle/entertainment journalist, then with one of the leading English newspapers in the country, I was fortunate to have had some fantastic opportunities, including meeting an incredible array of people, visiting exotic places and staying at some really swanky hotels and destinations.

To sweeten the aforementioned honey-coated deal at the L'ermitage, I was in Los Angeles to interview the cast of psychological thriller *Gothika*, which starred Robert Downey Jr and Halle Berry. He may not have been Iron Man back then, but it was still such a thrill to be interviewing the one and only RDJ! Charming, witty, handsome—Downey Jr was all of the above and more.

This soon became familiar to me. Interviewing famous people and jet-setting around the globe for interviews. There were a number of movie junkets to LA, New York, Tokyo, Taipei, London and Sydney during which I got to meet the likes of Chris Hemsworth, Tom Holland, Daniel Radcliffe, Tom Cruise and Nicole Kidman, and also pick the brains of my favourite directors such as Ron Howard, Baz Luhrmann and Cameron Crowe. Heck, I even visited Sesame Place in Pennsylvania and said hi to Big Bird, and there was this one time when Hugh Jackman took my hand and welcomed me to Australia. Yes, that actually happened, be still my beating heart!

I began working as an entertainment reporter in the mid 1990s. I was just a trainee then and earned a pittance but it had been a lifelong dream of mine to one day work in a newspaper office, with phones ringing off the hook and papers flying everywhere, just like in the *Mary Tyler Moore Show* and *Lou Grant* television shows I grew up watching. I was the only girl at school who listed 'journalist' as ambition at age nine, while most others wanted to be a doctor or lawyer.

Back in the days when I first started out as a cub reporter, what I enjoyed most was getting to meet all my favourite pop/rock idols. I not only got to interview Duran Duran in Hong Kong, Sting in Singapore, and Annie Lennox in Hong Kong, but also watched all of them perform live, as well as a host of other artistes, from N.E.R.D., the Killers and Muse to Bananarama and Cliff Richard, when he was a septuagenarian!

I love music and it was thrilling to be able to meet my idols and chat with them. The musicians I met were always very easy to talk to and laidback. They thought nothing of giving you an autograph or taking a picture with you. But this was not the case with the Hollywood fraternity in the 90s pre-social media era. Movie stars were a lot more guarded and had strict personal assistants or media liaisons who would stop you from pursuing a certain line of questioning that was too personal or from attempting to strike up friendly conversation.

Occasionally you'd get lucky and get a one-on-one interview but most of the time, you were lumped in a roundtable interview where journalists take turns asking the talent questions. It was a delight nonetheless to be a part of this whole rigmarole, and friends and family usually listened in disbelief when I shared anecdotes like how I'd had a few laughs with Tommy Lee Jones or had my picture taken with one of the snowy owls that played Hedwig. Or interviewed Brazilian footballer Ronaldo. (Not Cristiano folks, take it easy.)

That was back in 2006, when I travelled to Munich, months away from the FIFA World Cup and came up close with a bunch of footballers as well as swoon worthy German coach Juergen Klinsmann, when Nike launched one of its many editions of its Mercurial Vapor boots. On that trip, we travelled from Munich to Milan, via Venice, by bus and it was such a fun adventure with a large group of Asian journalists all travelling together. It didn't matter that I was a girl, the boys were such a sporting bunch and never once made me feel out of place. The World Cup, after all, has incredible universal appeal, and I remember connecting with so many people on that trip—men and women of all ages—because of our love for football.

There were spillover benefits too, as I got to see some great sites along the way, including the Rathaus-Glockenspiel clock tower in Marienplatz, Munich, and the Allianz Arena football stadium, the second-largest arena in Germany, even peeking into the changing rooms and warm up rooms! Our troop got to see how the football boots were made from scratch at the Nike factory in Montebelluna and it was the first time I'd really thought about how much science goes into something like making a boot! Not to mention what huge feet some footballers have, like Czech Republic striker Jan Koller who wears an EU size fifty-two!

Back home in Malaysia, I was on the entertainment and arts beat interviewing various artistes, from popstars the late Sudirman to Sheila Majid, and dance and stage personalities Jo Kukathas, Faridah Merican and Ramli Ibrahim. I enjoyed writing about the local English theatre scene, even though I was at first petrified after being chided by an actor for misquoting him! I admit I made a lot of mistakes but also learnt from them. It was a labour of love for me, because I saw so much passion and commitment in these talented individuals. I remember interviewing the first Malaysian Idol, Jaclyn Victor, even before she won her title, and watched as she ascended to the top of the Malaysian charts and hearts.

Life inside the office wasn't nearly as glamorous. We worked long hours, had to constantly meet deadlines and were always pushed to get scoops, deliver more and be faster than all the rest. Back in the early 1990s, there was no Internet, so research was done the old school way of looking through our archives of past articles, often having to wade through hundreds of paper clippings, or look through huge bound copies of old newspapers.

When I got married and decided to start a family, I moved to the subs desk so I would have more fixed hours of working. This turned out to be a blessing in disguise because I learnt so much of what went on in production and how the paper was put together from start to finish. In those days we still had paste-up artists manually cutting and pasting paragraphs together and we had to figure out what blends of CMYK to use in order to get a coloured headline!

I smile when I think about how far I've come, and what a wild ride it has been. After my children grew up and were of schooling age, I returned to writing, my first love. In the late 90s and throughout the 2000s, more and more opportunities started popping up for the media to go beyond our borders for interviews. Asia was a growing market, and we were often invited to cover everything from movies and music, to tourism, beauty and technology.

Thanks to my job, I was forced to and learnt how to travel solo. I also had to learn to speak to strangers, fight to be heard in a crowd, ask probing questions and really listen when people had a story to share, then make it palatable enough for anyone to read. I don't remember ever feeling discriminated against for my gender or race when out in the field. While I was overseas, however, I would worry about my spoken English, or rather Manglish, afraid that I would fumble with my questions or make a fool of myself in front of a star.

Even though I was nervous, I simply loved that I could peek into the lives of rich, famous and successful people and glean tips, or fashion articles out of these brief glimpses of very extraordinary craftsmen, CEOs, models and entertainers. And there were always other perks.

In Paris, France, I once got a luxurious spa treatment when I visited the skincare brand Clarins' head office on Rue Berteaux Dumas in Neuilly-sur-Seine. That came hand in hand with interviewing the Clarins brothers, sons of Clarins' founder Jacques Courtin. During this trip, they wined and dined me with champagne and a Bateaux-Mouches cruise on the Seine, and we also visited a gorgeous arboretum, where the herbs, plants and cultivars used in Clarins' products are grown.

When the Crown Casino in Melbourne, Australia relocated to the south bank of the Yarra River in 1997 and opened with a bang, guess who was there? At the time, the Crown was the largest casino complex in the Southern Hemisphere and I got to view the penthouse suite for the high rollers . . . Plus, I had a private jacuzzi in my room! For opening night, there was a double-bill showcase by pianomen Elton John and Billy Joel.

While in Italy, I got to stay at the lush Baglioni Hotel Luna. Located a few steps from Piazza San Marco, in the very heart of Venice, this historic hotel dates back to the twelfth century and was built on the possible location of the Knights Templar convent. And when in Milan, I went in search of Leonardo Da Vinci's *Last Supper*, while the other journalists travelling with me preferred moseying down the quadrilatero della moda packed with high-end boutiques and brands like Prada, Gucci, Moschino, Versace and Bulgari.

I have swum with a Maori Wrasse (his name is Wally!) in the Great Barrier Reef in Australia; I have sailed on an America's Cup yacht, actually grinding and halting to turn the pulleys and raise the mast and sails, while Cindy Crawford posed for the cameras on the Hauraki Gulf, off Auckland's coast in New Zealand; I have white water rafted down a gorge and dipped my feet into an icy cold creek, tackled robber crabs, sheared sheep, celebrated Christmas in June in the Blue Mountains, and slept under the stars on a pontoon, out on the open Coral Sea.

On the flip side to these adventures, however, were the ones that gave me a reality check. One such assignment was when the International Committee of the Red Cross (ICRC) invited the Malaysian media to visit its headquarters in Phnom Penh, then travel overland to Battambang, in northwestern Cambodia, to see the work it was doing with landmine victims. It was a trip filled with places and people that I won't forget easily.

Unlike previous assignments, free time was spent visiting the Tuol Sleng Genocide Museum where I got a ghostly glimpse of Cambodia's dark past. It shocked me that some visitors took touristy photos, smiling and posing for the cameras in such grave surroundings. But it set the stage perfectly for what was to come next.

As I met and spoke with the people here, the story I was to write unravelled itself, and this assignment turned out to be a truly enriching experience for me. I met people with disabilities who had benefited from

ICRC's work, those who had been fitted with prosthetic limbs and those who had gone on to start working despite their disabilities. There was even a women's basketball team on wheelchairs, who came out to play just for us!

I clearly remember meeting Sum Reth, a fifty-three-year-old man with one arm and one eye, who told me how he had lost his limb when he was ten, trying to escape a bomb falling from the skies during the Vietnam War. What struck me about him was that he could remain cheerful despite his hardships. He was elated that he was getting a new prosthetic arm after six years, and that it would help him in his work on his rice field. How could he not be happy, he asked me, now that there was peace across his country. His demeanour and simple words caught me off guard. And his words are still able to tug at my heartstrings.

Another part of the trip was getting to see how the Cambodian Mine Action Center (C-Mac) workers carry out their work. Cambodia is one of the most heavily mined countries in the world, with an estimate of nearly four to six million mines and other kinds of unexploded ordnance (UXOs) left over from the bombs dropped there by the United States in the late 1960s and early seventies. Even today, there are landmine victims registered annually—the thought that someone in this day and age can step on a landmine or bomb left behind fifty years ago is horrific.

The media was given a 'tour' through an active zone in the Traeng commune, in the Battambang province, where more than 800 villagers live. Here, the twenty-two members of C-Mac, including two women, meticulously free hundreds of square kilometres of land from these landmines and explosive remnants, every day under a blazing sun.

Geared up in a safety vest and protective headgear, it was exhilarating and a little scary to accompany them while they worked. The team had already uncovered two AP-mines, eight unexploded ordnances and 412 fragments of mines in these parts. They turn up every day to make sure their fellow countrymen will someday feel safe to roam about freely. Something I had taken too much for granted until then: the ability to take a stroll outside my own home without having to consider that I might accidentally step on an explosive device of some sort.

I was surprised to find that the many years of interviewing celebrities had given me a quiet conviction to bravely approach this very different, and difficult, subject matter. And while writing it, I was reminded of how people lead such varied lifestyles across the globe. I was grateful then, as I am now, that my job as a journalist has presented me a wide spectrum of experiences that I otherwise almost certainly would never have had.

A large portion of the days of my life has been filled with writing many cover stories as well as little announcements, thinking up headlines and choosing photos that complement my stories, thinking about white space and readers' attention spans. But I have also loved every minute of being in the field and I have learnt so much, as well as grown in confidence and character (I hope)!

Thankfully, I was able to bring up two wonderful children, all while holding down a very demanding job and I worked hard to move up the ladder. Twenty-eight years after I first joined as that wet-behind-the-ears trainee, I left my full-time job and the office . . . but I continue looking for opportunities where I can find a good story and wield my pen again!

The Death of a Stranger

By Lee Mylne

Her name was Maggie. A woman I barely knew whose accidental death changed my life in ways I could not have imagined when we both set out on a journey I'd often heard referred to as 'the trip of a lifetime'.

As a travel journalist, I am fortunate to see and experience places that many people never have the opportunity to reach. In many cases these travel experiences are hosted or sponsored by tourism or travel organizations or operators.

It was on just such a trip that I met Maggie. We were fellow passengers on an expedition cruise along Australia's Kimberley coast, from Broome in Western Australia to the Northern Territory capital, Darwin. Over ten days, we were to be travelling through some of Australia's most remote and spectacular wilderness, a 'soft adventure' in which I was taking part as a guest of a cruise company, to write about my experience for a national newspaper's travel pages.

By the third day, the forty-eight passengers were becoming accustomed to the wake-up call of the anchor chain rattling and the ship's engine starting. Slipped under our cabin doors each morning, a newsletter outlined the day's activities. On this day, it promised a morning swim in Crocodile Creek, so named for its rock formation shape, rather than reptilian inhabitants, followed by the possibility of exploring Dugong Bay, and continuing to Talbot Bay and Horizontal Falls. By mid-afternoon, the ship was at anchor and preparations were being made for our excursion to the higher reaches of Talbot Bay and the excitement of Horizontal Falls.

The Kimberley Coast experiences some of the largest tidal ranges in the world, reaching more than ten metres. One of the most extreme examples of this is Horizontal Falls, known to the traditional owners, the Dambimangari saltwater people, as *Garaangaddim*. The 'falls' are two sets of fast and powerful tidal flows, flanked by high ochre cliffs. The tides rush through two narrow gorges in Talbot Bay in the Buccaneer Archipelago, and reverse as the tides turn. The rushing tide, to the Dambimangari, is *Woongudd*, the creator snake. The first gorge is about twenty metres wide, water from the upper basin rushing through, creating a waterfall effect and eddying rapids. Access to the second set of rapids is between an even narrower gap in the cliffs, about ten metres wide. The effect of the waterfalls is created by the tide building up in front of the gaps faster than it can flow through them and there can be a four-metres high waterfall between the bays. The waterfall phenomenon has been described by David Attenborough as 'One of the greatest natural wonders of the world', according to the tourism promotion literature.

This is one of the popular highlights of cruising the Kimberley coast, as tourists thrill to a boat ride through the gaps between the cliffs to the bay behind. Donning lifejackets, we took turns to clamber into the two inflatable boats which accompanied the tender from the ship. One boat takes two passengers and the driver, the other takes four passengers. I was in the first to head out, along with a fellow traveller, a retired doctor whose wife was not keen on taking part. 'Hold on tight,' ordered our driver, as we approached the first set of rapids. We complied, bouncing about as we headed 'up' through the eddying water to the calmer bay above it. Each boat had its turn through both sets of rapids, our cameras snapping each other as we waited for the other to pass through, then we zipped back through and returned to the tender for others to take their turns. I was slightly disappointed, having been through other rapids on my travels, in jet-boats and white-water rafts. These seemed just a trifle tame, not quite living up to the hype, in my eyes.

'Did anyone not get a big enough thrill? There's room for one more in the last boat for anyone who wants another turn,' called our expedition leader. Quicker to respond than I was, my cabin mate hurriedly donned a lifejacket, ready to take up the vacant spot when the boat returned.

Suddenly, there was pandemonium. As the boat returned, one of the passengers was screaming 'Accident! There's been an accident!'. There was an immediate call for a doctor, and the man who had taken the ride with me hurried forward. I looked down from my seat on the open tender to see a woman's body lying in the bottom of the inflatable, partly shielded by those standing up as they came alongside. All I could see was a green t-shirt and a pair of legs. Who is it? Are they OK? What's happening? There was confusion on the tender, making it hard to work out what has happened. The couple in the other inflatable clambered aboard the tender, looking shaken and distressed. The woman was sobbing, her husband sitting silent, his head in his hands.

The two-passenger inflatable had flipped, tipping its occupants into the churning currents. The driver and male passenger had been pulled from the water by those in the second boat, but for long minutes Maggie was nowhere to be seen. When she surfaced from the roiling water, the others had struggled to get her into the inflatable. Another passenger began immediate CPR and mouth-to-mouth resuscitation as best he could in the difficult conditions, and the boat sped toward the tender on which we waited. Radio contact was made with the ship, the inflatable soon heading for its fast bearing Maggie and the doctor.

We bobbed in the tender on Talbot Bay, shocked and silent. Someone said: 'There, but for the grace of God . . . ' I am thinking, as I'm sure others are too: *It could have been me. It could have been any one of us.*

Resuscitation attempts continued on the ship's deck for more than an hour, while the rest of us stayed on the tender, away from the ship in a quiet inlet at the end of Talbot Bay, distracted by the geography, the splashes of colour from the Kimberley 'rose' flowers and scarlet claws of male fiddler crabs on the muddy banks. Despite the best attempts of the doctors on board, assisted by the crew, Maggie did not regain consciousness and died before we returned.

Our ship remained at anchor until the police arrived the next day from the nearest town, Derby, to investigate the accident. A day later, they took Maggie and her grieving partner with them.

That we had only just met Maggie belies the impact her death undoubtedly had on forty-eight strangers. We barely knew Maggie;

we barely knew each other. The journey we embarked on had not turned out the way we expected. The death of a stranger in this most remote and lovely part of the world affected us all. Some who were involved in the rescue and attempts to revive Maggie needed to talk it out. Some quiet conversations went beyond the polite exchanges we expect with new acquaintances.

With an average passenger age of seventy-two, there was a lot of history here and I drank in the stories and wisdom of these 'elders'. We shared fractured pieces of our lives, other journeys. Personal stories, terrors and traumas tumbled out. A long-lost daughter, found again. A child who died. Loves won and lost. A retired bank teller told me she had been held up at gunpoint three times. The things that have shaped us. Books, music, movies. Politics. Global warming. Behind it all was a shared sense of the sudden awareness of the fragility of life. Those unspoken words again: *It could have been me.*

There is no doubt in my mind that the effect of this terrible accident was intensified by the natural raw power of this ancient landscape. Beneath the picture-postcard scenery lie the dangers inherent in such a wild, remote and unforgiving place. As the cruise continued, and our schedule resumed some normality, there was a guilty pleasure in enjoying ourselves again. Under cloudless cobalt skies, we travelled through a landscape shaped over millennia, with sweeping watercourses, fractured chasms and stone walls, hidden crevices and overhangs, the 'cathedrals of the earth' as our expedition leader terms them; a description it's hard to argue with. We cruised sheltered river reaches heading for King George Falls, dwarfed by towering sheer red and gold sandstone cliffs on both sides, forged around 1,800 million years ago. This is an ancient, untouched place, vast and timeless.

The youngest of the passengers by some years, I was also something of an interloper. As a freelance travel journalist, I was being hosted by the cruise company to write about my trip in order to promote the following year's cruise program. From the outset, I had not kept this from the other passengers. It is part of the Code of Ethics I work under as a member of the Australian journalists' union, the Media Entertainment and Arts Alliance (MEAA), that journalists on assignment should 'Identify yourself and your employer before obtaining any interview for publication or broadcast'. At dinner on the first night, my table began the usual round of introductions. Hearing I am a journalist, one of the men at the table spat out: 'In my opinion, all journalists are liars!'

I chose not to engage in an argument; in my long career I've heard this kind of thing before and I dispatched him with a few polite but well-chosen words. In the short silence that followed, his wife leaned toward me and said: 'Good for you!'. Others at the table adroitly turned the conversation to the nature of reviewing and criticism, comparing travel writers to theatre reviewers, food critics and similar writers. I also work under the Code of Ethics of the Australian Society of Travel Writers, of which I am a Life Member and former president. That code requires members to act as travel critics, 'as ready to criticize as to praise'. Eventually we moved on to safer topics, but the exchange still sat heavily with me and in the days following Maggie's death I steeled myself for any more criticism of my profession that might come my way. If my presence is unwelcome, it might be a long voyage and already I was wondering how or what I could write about this trip.

Would some passengers believe I see this as a sensational story—in the worst sense of the word? That having a journalist on board would mean the story of Maggie's accidental death will be splashed across newspapers around the country? I realized, too, that the crew and the cruise company may be wondering about adverse publicity. I explained to the expedition leader that I am at a loss to know how to deal with this story, and hope he's taken it in, given the stress he is already under. As we are in remote country, with no internet or phone access, it's academic until we return to land in Darwin anyway.

Restless while waiting as the police conducted their interviews, I headed to the ship's forward lounge, where I encountered the doctor who had worked so hard to resuscitate Maggie. 'What will you write about this trip?' he asked. I honestly don't know, I confessed. His response surprised me. 'I think you should,' he said. 'I think this is a great story for you, and one that should be told.' I agreed but confessed I didn't know where to start. There are many ethical issues to consider.

Before the cruise, like all passengers, I was required to get a doctor's certificate stating that I was fit, outlining any medical conditions, and acknowledging that I would be in remote areas, far from any medical services. I was made aware that there would be no ship's doctor on board. The booking form included a waiver, which I happily signed. 'I am aware that your adventure trip, in addition to the usual dangers and risks inherent, has certain additional dangers and risks, some of which may include: physical exertion for which I may not be prepared, weather extremes subject to sudden and unexpected change, remoteness from normal medical services, evacuation difficulties if I am disabled. I accept all the inherent risks of the proposed adventure trip and the possibility of personal injury, death, property damage or loss resulting there from.' We sign these waivers without thought. After all, it won't happen to me. And if it does, I've got insurance. In the worst case, I'm a bit of a fatalist . . . if my time is up, it's up. If I worried about accidental death, I'd never go outside my front door.

Confronted with reality, and our own mortality, things looked different. My elderly companions' hearts and minds were open to challenges beyond their aging bodies. But soft adventure is designed by people much younger and is—to some extent—a matter of perception. What is easily within the capabilities of some may be beyond others. To cruise the Kimberley Coast without going ashore would be to miss the grandeur that captivated us; to miss the essence of the land. But the responsibility lies heavily on those who have care of their clients. We've seen the strain on the ship's crew and expedition leaders.

Nearly a decade later, I began to analyse the ethics of my craft as I returned to university to undertake a professional doctorate. This experience in the Kimberley has remained with me as one of the greatest ethical challenges I have faced in my career. On returning, my editor was unwilling to publish a story which had legal issues; the coroner's report into Maggie's death was still pending. Ethically, I could not write about the cruise as if the accident had not happened. But it would be unfair to the cruise company to criticize it for a freak accident. The ethical implications swirled in my head, and in the end, I did not write about it for the mainstream media.

In 2020, as part of my doctoral research, an interview with another travel journalist brought these memories and the ethical dilemma that swirled around that trip flooding back. My colleague had discovered while researching the Horizontal Falls that the Dambimangari traditional owners now request visitors do not negotiate the falls by boat when the tide is rushing. Traditionally, travel through the gorge was made only on the neap tide, when the water was calm; today's visitors seek the thrill of going through when the tide is rushing, ignoring or ignorant of the danger this creates. The Dambimangari believe that this potentially dangerous place must be treated with respect and consideration, to ensure safe passage for those who choose to enter it. For them, it is disrespectful—as well as dangerous—to travel through the falls at rushing tide and the *Woongudd* spirit is damaged every time people drive boats through the gap. It is a similar stance to that of the traditional owners of Uluru, who campaigned successfully for a ban on climbing the sacred monolith.

Such cultural sensitivities are among the many ethical issues that travel journalists must consider. Travel journalism is not always the lightweight 'entertainment' or lifestyle journalism that many perceive it to be. Journalists working in this genre must be as mindful of their ethical obligations as any of their mainstream colleagues. In the case of writing about Maggie's death at Horizontal Falls, my ethical considerations related to the concepts of fair reporting, but there are many other ethical issues which travel writers are increasingly considering when choosing destinations and travel products to write about.

It is hard to find words to describe the Kimberley. It is unutterably, savagely beautiful. It is a place that fills our souls and the empty places inside us, and drenches our minds with its solitude. I felt small in such a vast, timeless place.

I knew the lessons of this trip were important; every event and every conversation had its place and its meaning. Could I ever be the same after experiencing this, after being in this raw, untouched place? Could I ever explain its impact to anyone else?

Returning to city life, I felt blue and bruised. As my taxi from the airport sloshed through rainy streets on a cold, dark evening and the city lights came into view, a sense of desolation gripped me. It seemed dirty, ugly and noisy.

The journey to the Kimberley that I embarked on all those years ago impacted my life in ways I could not have foreseen. Life and death came together to change my way of thinking about my profession and my responsibilities. It made me value my life and how I should lead it. For me, it was so much more than just another travel story.

ALT TROPICANA:
The Underground Fashion World
of Cybercity Singapore

By Niki Bruce

Flying into Singapore at night I always felt that I had somehow slipped into the future. The glistening reflections of the city's twinkling lights in glossy puddles from the always recent rain, shine up at ancient trees painstakingly spotlit with energy-saving LED lights.

No matter the time I arrived, I'd be welcomed by sparkling clean spaces, glittering technology and the polite indifference that Singaporeans do so well. A nosy taxi uncle might ask me about my love life, or question where I had arrived from, before dropping me off at my heartland apartment block, often complete with a funeral being held in the void deck on the ground floor. I would be home; safe and comforted by the efficiency of my tiny island home.

I've had a lifelong relationship with the Little Red Dot. As a child my family would transit through Singapore on our way to our expat life in Kuching, Malaysia. Like all Australians, I would fly through Singapore on my way to the rest of the world, or stop off on the way back for a spot of shopping. Eventually I moved there after an unexpected and seemingly random job offer. I have been a journalist of sorts for years, bluffing my way through jobs as unlikely as editor for a slightly illegal English language publication in Beijing, creator of a pull-out magazine dedicated to regional horse-racing, and finally as an official journo in an actual newsroom. Saying 'yes' to a copy editor position for a national newspaper seemed an easy choice, considering it would get me out of countryside purgatory and back into Asia, the hometown of my dreams.

I've always said Singapore offers the best of everything one could want when choosing a hometown. It's clean, safe, technologically advanced, has great food, fabulous shopping, and a relatively good environment considering it is a comparatively tiny island. Sure, I might hate the weather—either hot and wet, or hot and dry—but that doesn't really matter when I can walk from one end of Orchard Road to the other completely indoors, never having to actually experience the steamy heat that encases this tropical country. I could travel from my apartment in air-conditioned comfort via underground transit tunnels and stations to any part of the island, without ever having to go above ground. In Singapore I would stroll through huge, geodesic domes of alpine plants. In Singapore, I could ride a gondola around a massive underground shopping complex threaded with artificial rivers, I could try a spot of ice-skating; all in a country that literally sits on the equator.

It sounds like the future, doesn't it?

The Little Red Dot of my experience sits at the end of the Malay Peninsula, a secular republic of many races surrounded by some of the largest Muslim populated countries in the world. As a uni student studying a range of random arts subjects, none of which ironically were related to becoming a journalist, Singapore was a source of fascination. So close to my homeland of Australia, which I endured as a teenager, pining for my more exotic past homes in Asia, Singapore was a dream town offering an escape from the sports-obsessed land I found myself forced to endure. For me, Singapore's history of invasion, colonization, rough independence and trade, was hypnotic. An *entrepot* for European and Asian nations for centuries, the gateway to the mystical 'East', the small island nation had always punched above its weight in many ways. Sure, Singapore wasn't perfect, despite my juvenile obsession. Its unique national character, at once driven and proud, is also conversely conformative and conservative. Although nominally secular, the people of Singapore are intrinsically religious, family oriented, generally risk averse, accept personal discomfort for the betterment of all, and believe in the importance of community. To stand out is to be *hao lian bo la liang*, a show off. To make a point of physically looking different, to wear 'interesting' fashion, to dye your hair or be openly homosexual, is not something many Singaporeans aspire to. For the majority, showing off should be restricted to the 'Four Cs'—car, condo, credit and country club membership.

So while I've always loved Singapore, it's not generally what you would call a home for cutting-edge, underground fashion which I also love. My love for fashion started early with my mother's handmade dresses in matching patterns with my sister—she always got red, I always got blue. Then I graduated to choosing my own clothes—as a tween I was big into colour matching—but that all changed once I discovered clubbing and Goth. Yes, I am an old school, hardcore Goth from way back. I once lived in a share-house with a guy who swore he was a vampire and slept hanging upside down using one of those weird ankle exercise machines from the eighties.

But back to Singapore. By the time I arrived to work in the island city I had years of fashion loving behind me. I was dedicated to my divine idol Yohji Yamamoto, I was obsessed with Tokyo, I had years of experience in Beijing chasing the club scene and its emerging fashion industry. Then I ended up working behind a news desk in the safest city in Southeast Asia. Yes, there was lots of shopping, but where was the fashion?

Singapore is known as the best place to shop in Southeast Asia. Its high-tech malls, marble-clad temples to consumerism, offer brands from Europe and the US, as well as from around the region. For about five years before I relocated, I flew to Singapore for my annual shop, looking for 'fashion' not just shopping for clothes. 'Fashion' is mostly a personal and aesthetic choice, it's your way of showing people who you are. Shopping is what you do to get your fashion. Singapore does not immediately come to mind when people talk about fashion as in having its own fashion DNA, but it definitely does if you are discussing shopping.

When I think of Singapore and the friends I made there, I realize that everyone I know, everyone I would actually name 'friend', I met through the fashion industry. I didn't arrive in the world of fashion in the usual manner. I wasn't a fashion obsessed tween or Vogue reading teen. Sure, I liked clothes - I even had a part time job in a 'dress shop' as they were called then—but I also did other things. Somewhere along my life line, however, I realized the difference between clothes and fashion. I discovered that I wanted to stand out, I wanted to look different. I wanted to be 'hao lian bo la liang'. Perhaps I would have been better off moving to Tokyo or Seoul? Singapore, after all, isn't exactly what you would call a fashion capital.

In 2019, I came across an article that claimed that Singapore was the thirteenth 'most fashionable country in the world'. I was gobsmacked. I sent the link to my friend Debra Langley—a Singapore-based fashion industry veteran with experience from the top end of the fashion world, down to the most cutting edge of fashion and technology investment and innovation. Like me, Deb was flabbergasted. Her reply went something like: 'You have got to be kidding!'. We riffed on our reactions, agreeing that the definition of 'most fashionable' was the sticking point. I asked another mate, top Singapore stylist Randolph Tan what he thought about it all. As expected, Randolph also scoffed and agreed with Deb and I that 'most fashionable' should be determined by originality. 'When we think of the majority of the Singapore population, we think of t-shirts and jeans or shorts, something that was influenced by American casual clothing, and not really specifically Singaporean,' he pointed out. We all ended up agreeing that while Singapore is probably the most 'shop-able' country, it isn't the most 'fashionable'.

I have always felt that there is an odd cultural cringe at work in the Singaporean population, which does not, on the whole, buy Singapore fashion brands. I realized after I became the editor of a women's fashion magazine website, that if a Singapore brand does not fit into a buyer's definition of a 'value buy' (cheap fast fashion) or is not an internationally respected high fashion brand, then it's not going to be popular. Unlike the majority of the Singaporean fashion media, I actually thought it was rather sad that Singapore-made fashion wasn't supported or celebrated. I once received an effusive email from the CEO of a major Singaporean brand thanking me for featuring it. I was rather surprised. Why wouldn't I support a major Singaporean fashion brand as a member of the Singaporean fashion media? Apparently this wasn't the 'done thing'. Singaporean fashion media focused more on imported 'luxury' brands because they brought more advertising. To me, this was an example of Singapore's cultural lack of self-confidence. During the early 2000s, the only time that I saw the Singapore fashion media supporting local brands was during the National Day celebrations in the month of August. A tired handful of local brands—usually the same ones—would be dragged out for a single story in the fashion mags.

I put this tendency to ignore home-grown fashion labels down to the history of the Singapore fashion industry. Reaching out to the OGs of the Singapore scene like Daniel Boey—who I named the godfather of Singapore fashion—and Peter Kor, I learnt that there had been a number of quality home-grown fashion labels in the 1980s and 1990s, but there were also an equal number of younger retail brands producing rubbish quality clothes. If you did buy a local piece or two, they often fell apart which meant that many buyers wouldn't go back. Then came the economic crash of 2008 and many of the more established Singapore brands went bankrupt or just closed up shop. In one of my very first Singapore fashion interviews, Peter told me about having to move overseas and work as a 'white label designer' making patterns for cheaply produced factory clothing in order to pay off his debts after going bankrupt. He never really recovered. His once substantial business has been compacted into a single atelier where he creates limited bespoke garments - basically working as a tailor when all is said and done. Once the money started coming back, the brands suddenly discovered they had been superseded by cheap, fast fashion and high street brands or the arrival of mid-range and high-end labels from around the world. Locally designed and produced fashion brands were priced out of the market.

By the time I arrived in Singapore in 2008, a whole range of new Singaporean fashion brands had popped up. One of them, Ong Shunmugan, is now considered to be one of Singapore's most successful fashion labels. It is lauded for its innovative mix of traditional Asian fabrics with modern shapes. Its products are beautifully finished with French seams; its sizes are correct; its fabric quality top notch but this production, proudly all made in Singapore, is only possible because the designer Priscilla Shunmugam created her own atelier of retired Auntie seamstresses and then had them trained in the traditional couture finishes she required. Why is this so important to note? Well, there are no fabric mills in Singapore. There are no sample factories. There are very, very few apparel production factories and they are only able to produce very small runs or very generic, low quality products. And the costs are more than double what you would spend in other Asian nations like Indonesia, Thailand, China or even South Korea. Even a major Singapore fashion label like the now defunct Raoul had to create its own pattern cutting studio and had issues securing the right hardware for its pieces. Although it was a large brand by Singapore standards, compared to international brands it was tiny. Raoul did not have the finance to create its own hardware; but neither could it buy in bulk in order to get exclusivity for a particular item. Stuck between a rock and a hard place the brand sometimes had to compromise, and these issues were a major part of its failure.

I relay these somewhat dry points in the hope that it can help explain why being an independent, creative fashion brand in Singapore is so hard to maintain. You can't just launch a label and expect it to succeed. The world of fashion has always looked glamorous from the outside, but from the inside it's a life of grudging hard work, never enough money, tossing up whether or not to pay the electricity bill or to eat. For designers the answer is always to pay the bill rather than to eat. Why do you think they're all so skinny? Even boring things like population size impacts on whether or not a fashion brand succeeds. Think about it. If your total population is only 5.89 million, of which less than half are female—the most likely to shop for clothes—and then of that fifty per cent less than ten per cent are even interested in 'fashion', your customer base becomes tiny. If your designs are even slightly left of centre, then the chance of your business actually making a profit becomes miniscule.

Yet, despite these seemingly insurmountable odds, there is, and has always been, a movement of alternative individuals in Singapore who have subtly made a statement that differs from the vast majority of the slipper-shod, shorts-wearing, singlet-ed population. There are people like me and my friends who defied the reality of forty Celcius temperatures to wear layers of Yamamoto-inspired black; other friends who relished the oversized and oddly embellished items of a Comme Des Garçons wardrobe; yet more friends who clomped around the MRT in Doc Martens boots or towering Tokyo toki-doki platforms. In Singapore, I even met a sadness of Goths, albeit of a relatively small number. For a cybercity that reeks of everything technological, electronic, virtual and digital, Singapore is also home to a motley collection of underground originals. Individuals that are iconic for choosing to hao lian, and show off their personal style.

I can't remember exactly when I met Kenny Lim and Andrew Low, two people who became my best friends in Singapore. Although we didn't obsessively text each other, or share every detail of our lives - in fact we never even visited each other's homes—we were always perfectly in sync with our personal style, our love of wearing black and our fascination with first G-Dragon, and now with *Word of Honor*. Kenny and Andrew are the OGs of Singapore's underground fashion movement. They founded the iconic alternative, non-gendered fashion brand called Depression, then later opened up Sects Shop (say that fast and you'll realize how clever that name is). These two are the loveliest, yet most intimidating-looking people I know. I also totally adore them.

According to the Depression myth, Kenny and Andrew met twelve years ago in the advertising industry, and after toiling for five to six years in a corporate and cutthroat environment, felt depressed with their lives and lifestyle. They decided to leave their financially comfy jobs to pursue a dream that would make them happier, launching Depression in 2006. This new 'job' is one that they say they still look forward to doing every day. A job that they would not feel depressed about all the time. Naming their first small fashion collection Depression was also a reminder that they wouldn't have to be depressed with their lives . . . and also a reminder that if you don't like the way you're living, you have the power to change your life. As a brand that began as t-shirts for the impoverished junior industry creatives and hairstylists of Singapore, Depression has now grown into a fashion label that has a distinct DNA, is stocked globally and has shown at Berlin Fashion Week. Depression is not a brand for everyone, but I love it. It's mostly black, drapey, oversized, punk-influenced streetwear for individuals who work in the creative industries and women like me who don't like wearing pink lace dresses.

Meeting Kenny and Andrew introduced me to the small, but feisty, world of Singapore's underground fashion and lifestyle scene. Home to a hodge-podge of punk and emo, gay and questioning, drag and trans individuals who generally hated Singapore for all the reasons I first came to love it. What I saw as safety, they saw as repression. What I saw as technological development, they saw as big brother. What I experienced as a comfortable, easy life as an expat, they experienced as classism, racism and homophobia. Meeting the underground opened my eyes to the way Singapore's intrinsically conservative culture restricted, repressed, restrained and even goaled people who were simply trying to express themselves. The underground was small, secretive and isolated, but I wanted to be a part of it in any way I could. Over the years I would hang out in the various incarnations of the Depression shop, eventually meeting members of the underground. But while I did what I could by writing articles about new independent brands, or highlighting young emerging artists, I was never really a completely signed-up member of Singapore's underground scene, no matter how I tried. At best I was a benign Auntie looking on from the outside, buying clothes I didn't need to support brands who were barely making ends meet.

Eventually Kenny and Andrew grew into a new home, a substantial 800 sq ft boutique called Sects Shop, on Orchard Road, the most conventionally successful place to shop in Singapore. The store now stocks not only their vastly improved and expanded own brand but also items from some of the world's biggest underground labels like Rick Owens, Telfar, Walter Van Beirendonck, and Raf Simons, plus cutting-edge emerging brands from around Asia. Did they sell out? Well, yes and no. They became as successful as they could considering the limits of Singapore's shopping population. Rather than pushing only smaller, cheaper products, they bit the commercial bullet and became the source of high-end international alternative brands. Sects Shop became the home ground of alternative Southeast Asia with celebrities and fans from Indonesia, Thailand, Malaysia, Brunei, Vietnam and further afield making pilgrimages on a regular basis. Customers come not just for the fashion, but also to meet like-minded indie fashion fans, and if they're very lucky, to be served personally by Kenny or Andrew.

On the front rows of fashion weeks, Kenny and Andrew are always noticed. They are forever being shot in street style photographs, often asked to take photos with young fashion students who have stalked them from show to show during a packed fashion week in Seoul, Tokyo or Taipei. I loved being with them at the shows, they'd tell me what to wear, take me to the backstreet studios belonging to undiscovered fashion geniuses and always join me for a smoke between runway shows. We became a 'thing', one blue-haired white woman wearing black, hanging with two Asian guys with matching outfits and interesting hair. Kenny and Andrew have always been distinctly different, and always at least two seasons ahead of everyone else. Kenny always has a mohawk of some kind, he almost always wears all-black layers. Andrew's hair is always very, very short—sometimes coloured—and while he also wears a fair bit of black, he wears more colour than his partner. The two are of similar height, they come as a pair. Kenny talks more, he's the business and marketing side of the partnership; Andrew talks less, he's the creative, the designer, but when he does speak it's always on point, direct, and obeyed. Over their many years in business Andrew and Kenny have nurtured a dedicated band of staff who are just as important to the underground scene in Singapore as their bosses are. There is also something called the 'Depression Tribe', people who have been supporters of the brand, and Kenny and Andrew, since their first forays into fashion. I'm proud to call myself one of them.

Kenny and Andrew came first, then I met other members of the Singapore fashion underground. There was a short-lived but interesting incubator space in a shopping mall where graduate collections by students of Singapore's most interesting fashion school, Lasalle College of the Arts, sat next to crafty bits and pieces from hobbyists, for example. There I met Gilda Su, Shaf Amis'aabudin and Nathanael, the designers of Mash-Up, and Samuel Wong from the brand Evenodd. None of whom are in the fashion world any more, but all of whom were individuals happy to be hao lian. Through them I met Bobby Luo and Ritz Lim of Butter Factory fame, and creators of Superspace and

Yum Yum Disco Dong. In the early 2000s, this loose collective of queer creatives were the groundbreaking ancestors of the current generation of Singapore-based LGBQT+ and creative individuals. Offering a brighter, lighter and crazier way for young people to express themselves, this group lifted the spirits of all who encountered them, including me. The iconic Butter Factory nightclub owned by Bobby Luo in both its Singapore locations was the focus of all that was bizarre in club fashion, its regular theme nights and New Year's Eve parties saw the creation of gigantic costumes—the stars of the show always Bobby, and his partner Ritz Lim. These uniquely Singaporean fashion creatives came to congregate at the short-lived but well-remembered Superspace store that stocked a mix of local brands and quirky bits and pieces from international drag stars to cutting-edge Japanese visual kei designers. While both the club and the store are no more, those involved continue to make their marks in oddly underground ways—an organic pet food brand springs to mind.

The Singapore underground had yet more to offer. I remember seeing the first collection from avant garde designer Max Tan, and hailing him Singapore's answer to everyone from Comme Des Garçons' Rei Kawakubo, to the next Rick Owens. While Max has shown at prestigious arty fashion events like Amsterdam's modefabriek, and iconic model Carmen Dell'Orefice, formerly Salvator Dali's muse, has walked his runway show, Max Tan remains an underground brand barely eking out a living, despite his tenure of ten years, with a mix of award prizes and a mixed bag of collaborative collections. Like other talented Singapore designers, Max Tan is unlikely to become a household name. Another iconic Singapore designer Thomas Wee, who is described by those in the know as indisputably the very best Singapore fashion designer, is reaching his 80s and likewise has never become a household name. If we are lucky his work will be archived and saved in one of the country's modernist museums; if we're not, his work will be forever lost.

Over the ten years I spent in Singapore teetering between the commercial world of big media magazines and my preferred world of quirky underground fashion, I hope I helped some designers stay in business. I could list here another twenty or thirty brands and designers who created some sort of original fashion, most of whom would be recognized by only a handful of Singapore's fashion elite, none of whom will leave a lasting impression on the general clothes-buying public. But that underground fashion world still exists in juxtaposition to the glossy, neat world of Singapore's corporate conglomerates and scruffy Aunties and Uncles that inhabit the heartland homes of towering Housing Development Board apartment blocks. One might think I'd be depressed at the number of creative individuals and brands I've seen disappear in my limited tenure as a member of the Singaporean fashion media, but I'm not. Despite the fact that Singaporean fashion culture could be seen as an example of homogeneity winning at the price of individuality, there has always been reason for me to hope. Some of my best friends, and coolest experiences have been found in the quiet resilience and stubborn determination of the alternative fashion world ensuring there will always be another option for those who want to be hao lian.

Calling out the Caller

By Jayagandi Jayaraj

'*Could you go to your wardrobe, and look at your deck of panties and bras? Tell me. What colour are they mostly in?*'

His confidence was unwavering. Slightly authoritative but still matter-of-fact like he'd known this script by heart and practiced it a million times.

'*They're almost all in black.*'

I responded without any hesitation while getting myself comfortable on the sofa.

'*I see . . . but where are you now? Are you physically in your room, looking into the wardrobe? It's really important that you are.*'

There was an immediate frustration in his voice. Maybe even anger. Most definitely anger. It must have been such a turn-off that I wasn't crouched at my zip-up cupboard peering at laces and Lycra in black.

'*Look, I don't have to be. I know what's in my wardrobe, so believe me when I say they're mostly in black. By the way, this survey is getting way too uncomfortable. Are we even close to being done yet?*'

Of course, I did not owe him anything so I instinctively communicated my frustration over his seedy insistence to signal that it was not okay. I gave him a chance to end it, to see if he would back off.

'*Don't worry, Malar. Many women are often taken aback by these questions which are intimate. Your reaction is totally expected. These questions are perfectly normal to the nature of the survey, and it's really to enhance our future product offerings. The good news is, we are almost done. I've only got one more page to go.*'

Sensing my frustration, he gave me reassurance. But he had also addressed me by my *middle* name, which was super strange. Troubling, even.

Well, that was Richard. Oh wait. Thirty minutes earlier, he had introduced himself as a Steven, saying that he represented an international undergarment brand, conducting phone surveys on the wants and needs of women so the brand could improvise on its lingerie line. He was so sleek in his approach that I had bought into this story when he had first contacted me two weeks prior to this phone call. I was away in Singapore on a work assignment when he had first contacted me. Not willing to bear the international charges, I had declined the invitation. Like a well-trained market researcher, he apologized, and sought to speak to me on a convenient time and day. I left it at that, and forgot all about it.

The phone call eventually came, rather unexpectedly on that Friday night, pass 9 p.m. What an odd hour to be questioning a stranger on her underwear choices, was my immediate thought. He assured me that the company's research and development team worked till 2 a.m., and a late-night call was ethical for as long as the respondent consented to the time. To further strengthen his case, he added that the 'survey' targeted young adults including college and university students, but women up to the age of 64 had also been part of it. As a token of appreciation, he also promised me cash vouchers worth RM150 (about USD forty in early 2006), courtesy of the lingerie brand. That was his opening and introduction.

At this point, I was already suspicious of the survey storyline. For a few months after my graduation, I had worked as a market research officer for a market research firm. During that stint, I was trained to conduct phone surveys, on-site audits and interviews. I also learnt that phone calls after 9 p.m. was not a norm, and ringing a person for the same survey after a two-week gap seemed fishy, too. Besides, every phone survey I've conducted was within office hours, none past 6 p.m. These were the reasons why I was convinced that this conversation with Richard needed recording with a pen on my notebook. If someone was determined to take advantage of me in this way, I might as well probe the situation within my capacity as a journalist to see if there was any story in it.

Richard began with the basics; my vital statics and personal care routine. He didn't pause or hesitate with his questioning. Rather, he continued in a clinical style like how telemarketers generally did. He followed up with a string of well-planned questions that were presented with a set of choices. Those were the easy, direct ones, designed to have the feel of a real survey, and possibly to get to know his victims better and build a rapport with them. He also volunteered personal information about himself; his supposedly mixed parentage background, who his fiancé was, where she worked and when they planned to be married. By revealing this, he was painting a picture of himself as a committed young man, who was up late, merely doing his job. Up until this point, it felt easy and safe for me. Work as usual.

In the next two hours, Richard's questions would float between casual, moderately invasive, and downright sexually-explicit, interjected with firm assurances that they were meant for survey purposes. Whenever he felt like I was within his game plan, he threw in open questions like my take on premarital sex. The questions were gingerly phrased to sound almost neutral like questions posed in open forums to gather public opinion on general subjects. But there was nothing neutral about Richard's questions. In fact, they were willfully programmed to cross the boundary, tap into a woman's private space and assault them, just when they least expected it. His questions were friendly yet predatory, light yet dark and they felt like jabs to the head when I least expected it, leaving me disoriented for a while but also even more determined to get the work done.

As he continued to flip the pages of his 'survey', I flipped the pages on my notebook, maniacally scribbling down details as we spoke. My knuckles became stiff from it. My heart raced in anticipation and horror of what seemed like a never-ending stream of wrongful questions made to sound legit. I couldn't believe his audacity. Though it made me wildly uncomfortable and angry, I gritted my teeth and pushed out a general answer. Whenever I evaded a question, he brought it up again, and when I refused an answer, he grew impatient with me. I obviously wasn't an ideal target for him. Despite that, he stayed on because I hadn't hung up on him. Maybe there was still a glint of a chance that I'd give in to him. The call finally came to a frustrating end when I was unwilling to go on further. At this point, I had run out of juice to process his pace and we were really just going in circles. Judging from the tone of his voice, he was clearly annoyed with me, yet he had requested several referrals for female friends for the 'survey'. I gave out phone numbers of two close friends just to track his next move, and immediately after, he called one of them; only this time, his company was operational for twenty-four hours, and not till 2 a.m. like he'd told me earlier. Of course, I had also warned these friends right away about the caller, but we just didn't expect the call to come so soon after mine. By the time the call had ended, it was almost midnight. I finally stretched out of the couch and sat upright on the dining chair, staring at my notes which took up nearly half my notebook. I was numb from feeling so much from that call but my mind was also busy drafting that story.

I spent the next few days checking up on the information I had managed to gather from him. The national telco company confirmed that the phone number he had given me was untraceable. No surprises there. The international lingerie brand in question also issued a statement saying that there were no such surveys on their end. I just needed these to be addressed and confirmed for the story I was about to write. Getting the story published was important to me as a mean to alert future victims of this man. Although my primary reason for the story was to caution other women, what I got in return was much more than that. The article was published on a national publication I was with at that time, and it narrated the predatory nature of the conversation between Richard and I. There were also two more side stories to the feature. One, on profiling people like Richard through interviews with a criminal psychologist and the police, and another on how market research firms actually conducted phone surveys.

The saucy nature of the main story sure raised some eyebrows. A section front-page content with sexual elements was still sensational, and if the writer was a female, she was also open to judgement in some ways for it. After all, why would a respectable woman spend that many hours and knowingly entertain a call like that. A male colleague, someone whom I had considered a friend, came forward to seal this notion. 'You know what this makes you? This makes you a slut,' he sneered, with clear emphasis on the word slut, in front of a few others, at the common area we worked. The four or five pairs of eyes fixed on me were equally shocked as I was. I felt blood rushing to my face. Not sure if they were expecting a rebuttal, but I froze, lost for words. I did not see that coming, not from this colleague of all people. I was totally blindsided; shocked and betrayed at the blatant victim-blaming and labelling. For the first time after the call, I actually felt like a victim simply for having written that story. In the weeks to follow, he would speak to me about it, and apologize over the matter with me explaining why it was not cool to begin with, and why such stories needed to be told. My decision to follow up on the call, knowing full well what the caller's intentions were, was not a question of morality. As a journalist, I felt socially obligated to report the incident, as a way to alert future targets so they didn't fall victim to Richard or people like him. Or at the very least, it was going to be on record for future reference should there be a need for it. I'm glad that many saw it this way, and applauded me for it. Some even joked that I must have been bored enough to spend hours on that call. But there certainly was appreciation, and curiosity about the story, and that felt good.

What's most gratifying and eye-opening, post-publication were the emails and calls I had received from the other victims of, very likely, the same predator. I was convinced Richard was involved in those other cases due to the nature of the questions, and the pretext under which these questions came about; a survey for a beauty/ underwear/ women's product company. These women were able to relate and find stark similarities between my story and their experiences. Most called in to say that they'd encountered the same caller, and decided to cut him off. A couple of others admitted that they didn't suspect a thing until they got to the more explicit questions. Importantly, my story had meant that they weren't alone in this, and that they had nothing to be ashamed of because it wasn't their fault. It was then that I understood the gravity of his doing, and why the story was absolutely necessary. We were dealing with a predator among us, who had been operating boldly with a systematic plan, creeping up on more women than I had previously thought, making them feel less at some point about themselves, and even unsafe. He needed to be called out on his actions, no matter where he was hiding. Calls like this could push women into a dark place even for someone who was 'prepared' for it like myself. When the buzz around the article had settled, I did end up feeling unsettled over the saga. In the early days, the experience had pushed me to be suspicious of male friends and people I befriended. It didn't help that I kept meeting new people in my line of work. I incessantly wondered if the caller was someone within my personal circle, if he was a friend's friend or someone who just knew of me. I wondered if he had already known details about me even before he made that call, or how he had gotten hold of my mobile number. As a young journalist covering news and current events at that time, I had my name card printed with my personal mobile number on it so my contacts could reach me directly for breaking stories. Could he be one of the hundreds who had my name card? I wrecked my brain, trying to establish that evasive connection, if there ever was one. But the single most thing that really creeped me out was him addressing me by my middle name. To my knowledge, no one referred to me by my middle name except family, close childhood friends and those in my innermost circle back in my hometown, which was about 200 km away from Kuala Lumpur where I had relocated to. So, yes. I was both puzzled and horrified that he picked up my middle name with such ease and familiarity. No matter what I did, my thoughts kept circling back to these questions. As a result, I dealt with some form of anxiety. I coped with these difficult thoughts by dancing it out. The adrenaline helped to mask these thoughts. Over the years, I had managed to put that aside and move on, concluding that perhaps he had stopped, or his tricks had gotten old and that people were able to call his bluff. Little did I know that I would hear of him again.

Twelve years later, I would go on to work for a magazine publisher, managing content for a fitness magazine. It was particularly a busy day, where we were closing pages and wrapping up for the month. The editorial floor was quiet, but the hands and minds that occupy it were hard at work when all you hear were the sounds of fingers punching words into the keyboard against the steady whir of cool air blowing from the ceiling cassettes. I was clearing a stack of proof I had just received from the printer. It would be sent back to the printer after another round of checks by my editor-in-chief. When I was done with the stack, I gathered the glossy pages and scurried towards my editor's room on the other side of the editorial floor so I could get them ready for the printer by lunchtime. Nearing her room, I heard a commotion from within. There was some talk about an indecent caller.

'People have been contacting us to verify calls they've received from someone who claims he's one of us. Says he's calling for a survey, and later starts with lewd questions, 'exclaimed the editor-in-chief while hastily gathering her notebook and handbag to get to the police station.

Her eyes were livid in disbelief of the situation, and I immediately recognized it. He had struck again. The hair on my neck stood, my heart raced against every word from my editor's mouth. My own mouth went dry, and I remembered everything like it had happened just yesterday.

'I *know* this character, he's called me many years ago. This is his MO,' I told my editor. She stopped in her tracks, and eyed me in silence. Tell me more, she said. I yanked out my story in almost a single breath, and even gave her the links to my articles about it. She was completely flabbergasted by my account. I was, too. Again.

Was I naive to assume that an account of my experience with him in a newspaper would end this? I guess not. Maybe it even fanned his ego more than anything, but it was also refreshing to know that police reports against him and media references on him now exist. He is on the criminal radar, and *that* mattered. My intention was to alert victims and assure them that it was not their fault in a world where victims were mostly blamed for harassments of a sexual nature. The only person at fault here is the perpetrator, in this case it's Richard, Steven or whatever his name is now. It was exactly why I needed my pen and notebook on that day—to call him out, because I could, and I will continue to do that whenever necessary in my capacity to put a face to this person.

Who knows, it could be a familiar face from my Facebook.

Letters from Readers,
or Remembering that Writing
is to be Read

By Erna Mahyuni

It is strange being a journalist in the age of social media. When I was a child I would skim through newspaper pages and remarked the names I would see attached to the stories. Some names I would remember and some I would not but my attention was most held by, of all people, columnists.

Amir Muhammad had a column once in the *New Straits Times* and it was one I looked forward to reading then. I was a child but Amir was a young man, sharing his recollections of life in Kuala Lumpur including afternoon socials that seemed a world away from my simple life in a small suburb of sleepy Kota Kinabalu.

Now I am the columnist and Amir has gone on to filmmaking and publishing books. Decades after I read his column, I ended up auditioning for and getting a role in Amir's film *The Big Durian*. We became friends on Facebook.

I wrote a Facebook note once, mentioning how I grew up reading his columns and his laughing comment: 'You never told me!' But I did, in a way, on social media.

Saying I owe Twitter my career seems an exaggeration but it's not. A former boss reached out to me, set up a meeting and when I was hired, gave me a column.

The story is really not about the column but how I kept it. My column survived because it was read and that is the simple gist of it.

A problem most writers have is ego, a belief that their writing is so important that it must be read and should be read, that their words are so important they are untouchable and should not be sullied by the hands of a sub-editor.

What they do not understand is that editors, sub-editors and proofreaders are doing them a favour. For writing to be read, it must be readable. If it is not made palatable, how then can you expect to be read?

Not all writers have the gift of Umberto Eco or Gene Wolfe, writers who require a lot of effort if you want to get through even a chapter. Eco tends to be verbose and Wolfe has a penchant for using words long retired from modern lingua. Yet if you manage to get past the obscure vocabulary and layers of metaphors, the end result is some enjoyment and a real satisfaction once you get to the end.

It is not satisfying for readers to suffer the clunkiness of bad, unedited writing.

A writer who wishes to write only for themselves should perhaps stick to journaling or if they would like to chance a stranger finding their words then maybe they would be better off with a blog.

It is good to write what you love but a writer must write to be read.

At least, that is what a working writer must do.

It is why I owe social media a great debt because there is nowhere that gives you as immediate and as wide a test readership than social media.

Facebook is for the people who know you more intimately, the ones who are curious and sincere about wanting to know what you think or feel.

Twitter is for strangers who are harder to woo but quicker to react to a well-crafted sentence. I miss the 140-character limit because I think nothing has taught me the value of conciseness and brevity as well as writing a short tweet.

When you have a very hard word limit, you must be selective and particular about their impact. You must consider the likelihood of misunderstandings and the limitations of the medium.

It is too easy to get addicted to the rush of checking notifications and perusing replies, composing witty repartee (or so you believe it to be) and chasing validation.

What must be remembered is that tweets or Facebook posts are like ripples on the water that will come, go, and dissipate. There is no permanence to them and in the end, they are but tools.

Social media paved the way to my current path but what sealed it, I think, was a hug.

During my short stint with an online news site, I had volunteered to write about a hot button issue at the time. In January 2010, the weekly Catholic publication the Herald had petitioned successfully to the High Court to be allowed to use the word 'Allah'.

That ruling was overturned years later but at the time it caused tensions that led to attacks on churches, all over the use of a name.

'Why is your Allah not my Allah?' ran the headline of my piece and it earned me some manner of recognition as well as online abuse.

I felt compelled to write it at the time as I saw the argument over a word was a terrible result of decades of a lack of understanding of how minorities lived, as well as the dubious standard of theology teaching in the country.

What I wanted, desperately, was for the people who were saying that no one had the right to use a word but them, to understand that the word belonged to everyone who used it.

Instead, I got emails and comments from people thanking me for understanding but it wasn't me who needed to understand.

Days after the article was published, I met a friend who greeted me with a hug and told me she had not understood, before, what the word meant to people outside her race and faith. What I wrote helped her see what she couldn't before and she was thankful.

I do not know if there were others like her who, after being informed, looked differently at the issue. What mattered to me was that at least one person did.

There is a lot of talk about changing the world but sometimes, I think, you need to start by learning how to persuade and change just one person's mind.

Words have power, even more so in an age where information has become currency and companies profit from the sale and exchange of seemingly innocuous data such as what time we usually visit a mall for brunch.

It is why copywriters get paid a lot more than journalists as they are masters of persuasion in the service of profit.

During my short stint I had to sub-edit the work of columnists. It was good preparation for what would come later and I learned just how not to be a columnist.

One of them was all too aware that editing his columns was an act of torture and cheerfully admitted he wasn't much of a writer. Not that it made his over-long paragraphs and sentences that would run-on as long as a marathon any easier to proofread.

At the very least he never complained about my edits unlike one columnist he was convinced he was a gift to Malaysian journalism. I'd met journalists who complained that their work had been 'butchered' by sub-editors but after being a sub for over seven years I am convinced they had an overly high opinion of their own writing.

This guy certainly had; he was addicted to using words that had gone out of vogue in the last few centuries and when senior editors tried to reason with him, could he not try to make his writing more accessible, he protested.

He claimed he was helping improve the literacy of the Malaysian public and if they did not understand what he wrote, they should try harder.

Every day I had to sub his column I fantasized about making him eat his words. Preferably they would be printed onto waste paper, charred and stuffed into stale bread.

Once he was hired for some supposed exclusive coverage and he had one stipulation, which was that none of his copy would be touched.

I reckon only one publication put up with his utter crap as nearly a decade has passed and I do not remember his name, but I do remember he was an awful pain.

My current editor perhaps benefited from my experience as I have never questioned her judgement when editing my pieces and I consider myself lucky enough that her efforts have kept the column published, never spiked, and only heavily censored once.

'I wonder sometimes if you *want* to get arrested,' she said in the early days of my column when I was still trying to see just how far I could go before the heavy hand of the Information Ministry called my employers to complain.

Looking back, I think I was lucky. Lucky to have just been given a column (I hadn't asked for one, my then-senior editor just informed me I had one), fortunate to be allowed to write whatever I wished and been given years of practice, along the way, training myself to deliver a column weekly for the last nine years, only ever missing one week.

Writing for print does not have that immediacy of feedback. Each week I would write whatever I wanted, as much as I wanted and then waited to see the response.

My years as a magazine editor trained me to write headlines and to be mindful of my word count. It also taught me there is more to writing in the modern age than just putting words to paper.

A column was like a condensed version of a magazine minus the ads and headache of sorting page ratios in the way it needed to be packaged. Every column was an experiment, much like the way I tracked my twitter engagement metrics.

You discover that spending a little extra time on your headline matters but if you made it over-sensational, you risk upsetting your readers. You also learn some people do not actually want to read your writing as much as they just want to yell at you about your headline.

It sounds calculated, doesn't it? That it doesn't just flow from some fount of inspiration and it cheapens the act to care so much about how best to present your writing and make it palatable instead of being, oh, true to yourself.

There lies the mistake, really. If you care enough about what you write, if you deem it important enough to be put out into the world then why not expend effort to make sure it is read? If the words matter then why is it so wrong to care about such details such as headings or sub-headings, repeated words or clarity of sentence structure?

When I don't write columns, I write tech reviews and I write them as though I am writing for my editor. Not in the 'I am meeting my deadline and assigned topic' but my editor is of a generation where modern tech can be a challenge. I eschew jargon, skim over overly technical details that can really just be linked to online, and write as though I was talking to her about a new phone over coffee. If I can write it in a way she can understand, I believe that anyone can.

If you care enough about your writing and you care enough for the people who will read it, it comes across in the words. I've learned that from the e-mails and comments I have received through the years.

I keep a folder in my email where I save the ones I get from readers, even the creepy ones from a rather senior gentleman who really shouldn't be posting photos of my face so frequently on Facebook.

There's the email from the woman who finally made a mental health appointment after reading my series on mental health awareness. There's the note from the woman who shared her struggles after divorce after I wrote, pleading, for couples not to stay together just for the kids.

They email my work address, the long-timers and regulars, while the newer readers use Google to find my website where my contact form waits for them.

Making myself so accessible also means I open myself to the not-so-nice side of internet interactions. Writing about current affairs and often criticizing the government as well as certain politicians opened me up to the new attack dogs of the internet: cybertroopers.

Cybertroopers are a relatively new type of propaganda machine, people marshalled into promoting a specific agenda, usually tied to a government or political party, often both. They are not a secret in Malaysia, with their activities and funding exposed to the public years ago by disgruntled former cybertroopers.

Getting into the crosshairs of cybertroopers would mean a relentless flood of comments on every one of your social media accounts. It got so bad once after a particularly controversial tweet I'd made that I had to go private on Instagram and deactivate my journalist page on Facebook.

There was a time when the cybertroopers had left me alone, rumour was, because my sister was at the time a minister's aide and they'd been told to leave me alone.

If it wasn't internet comments it would also be emails. Death threats were at least a biannual thing and I'd had to document the many I received, just in case I would need to make a police report.

I do not think it would make a difference if I did; after all, critics of the government are unlikely to get protection from those hired by the government to harass them.

What matters more to me are the emails in my saved folder that remind me my columns are read. I am grateful for each time someone takes the effort to message me because it means they understood what I felt I needed to say.

I will never be a copywriter because I do not write what I think will move people or what they want to read. I write about things that I think matter enough to risk someone sharing a screenshot of my face on an ultra-right Facebook page and trying to dox me, and I do my best to make my words as easy to understand despite my limited talent.

There was once that ex-editor of mine was put on the spot at a public forum and asked who his favourite columnist was. He mentioned a name and said it was a pity how few people wanted to read said person's columns while 'Erna's gets hundreds, thousands of shares'.

At the time I felt slighted. It felt unfair to have someone say, in this case a superior, that my columns were the most read instead of someone who was apparently more worthy of eyeballs.

Yet in the end what mattered is that yes, I was reminded that people do read what I write. I am not preoccupied with how many or who because really, counting the shares and likes is but an exercise in vanity.

Perhaps I am lucky that in many of my letters I see the phrase 'thank you for writing' but in truth I feel as though I am the one who should be grateful.

Whether they get bouquets or brickbats perhaps writers should also learn to say a silent prayer of thanks whenever their works are read because in the end, isn't that the very point?

Poverty in the Time of Covid

By Zela Chin

When I met Mei and her well-behaved daughter, Ling, at their home, I noticed how Mei almost made herself smaller as she squeezed past her teenager to get something to show my cameraman. There were only two places to sit: the desk chair and the lower bunk bed. Ling was in the chair doing her homework and Mei was on the bed, so my cameraman and I talked to them from outside the threshold. The entire flat could be walked in five steps.

I was working on a story about how the pandemic was affecting Hong Kong families below the poverty line, so I visited Mei and Ling in their subdivided flat. It's an apartment that has been divided into smaller units. Theirs was one living room with a sink. It's all of 50 square feet and housed their earthly possessions: a bunk bed, a desk and a chair, a drawer, a TV, a metal shelf with kitchen utensils, and an electric burner. The adjoining toilet had a showerhead above it. Mei and Ling slept on the lower bunk, and used the top bunk for storage.

Although small living spaces are the norm in Hong Kong, I was still shocked at how cramped their flat was. There was barely enough room to turn around, let alone stretch out one's arms. The flat was so tiny that my cameraman had to film some of the shots from the threshold with the front door wide open.

Mei was from a rural province in China. She married a man from Hong Kong and gave birth in the mainland. When Ling was a month old, they moved to Hong Kong, but divorce came soon after. Mei had been raising Ling alone, and moving from one subdivided flat to another.

In my years as a journalist, it's not common for an interview subject to allow me and my cameraman an intimate view of their home life. And I can count the number of times I've been to a subdivided flat on one hand.

So I was embarrassed and uncomfortable to see Mei and Ling's tiny home. The mother and daughter pair were matter-of-fact about their living situation. To cover my confusion and ease my nerves, I spoke incessantly, and made a clumsy attempt at a joke, 'You two sleep together on the lower bunk, how cozy'.

Mei shared that she and her daughter would get in each other's way and argued often. I wondered where they went if they needed space to cool off. Would one of them be forced to sit in the bathroom to get some alone time?

I was shocked to learn that they rarely left their home because they only had a handful of face masks and didn't want to waste any. It was very difficult for everyone to source masks at the beginning of the Covid-19 outbreak. But by the time I interviewed the mother daughter pair half a year later, masks were plentiful and I had stocked up on boxes and boxes of face masks, so I could use a fresh one daily. They only had about 10 masks for about five days, and depended on the kindness of strangers for more.

Mei's biggest disappointment was Ling's grades had slipped during the pandemic. She used to be in the accelerated courses. Then her school changed to virtual learning, but Ling didn't have a computer and couldn't keep up with the coursework on her smartphone.

I cried inwardly when I heard this. Ling wanted to get good grades, go to a good university, land a good job so that she could buy a big house for her mother. Isn't that every immigrant's dream, to have a better life?

My parents immigrated to the United States for the same reason. And we believed in the American dream. I studied hard, got into Duke University, one of the top ten universities in the United States, and now I'm able to work abroad and live as an expat in Hong Kong.

While the pandemic had made my life uncomfortable, would it quash Ling's dreams completely? Would they be stuck living in a subdivided flat forever? At the very least, the pandemic was a major setback for the mother and daughter, and they would probably take years to recover from it.

Since January 2020, grocery prices at Mei's local market had gone up thirty per cent to 100 per cent, stretching her tight budget.

Mei and her daughter get by on US$950 a month in government subsidies. About US$575 went to rent and utilities, and about US$370 were allocated to food, school fees, and other expenses.

So Mei supplemented the budget with food handouts from a church in her neighbourhood. She went regularly and picked up cookies and packaged meals donated by convenience stores. Mei and her daughter would eat only one box each of meat and rice a day, and Mei would add fresh vegetables from the market.

The church serves underprivileged people, such as minimum-wage workers and recipients of government welfare. It used to give out free dinners to the congregation one day a week, but amid the pandemic, it handed out food twice a week because there was a need.

The reverend at the church said that because the pandemic was lasting longer than expected, more people were becoming unemployed. And that meant more people needed the food handouts.

To prevent the spread of coronavirus cases, the government restricted restaurants' opening hours and imposed rules to limit their capacity. That meant restaurant staff were working only one to two days a week, instead of five days like they used to. Bars, beauty salons, gyms, and karaoke rooms were also closed for months at a time.

The reverend worried that the church's beneficiaries would not be able to withstand the pressure. Many would have no income to pay rent, and they were stressed; some had mental health problems. So besides handing out sustenance, the church volunteers also provided friendship and emotional support.

My heart sank when I heard all this. I read the newspaper headlines, and I saw that the unemployment rate kept rising, but to actually meet the jobless and see them scramble for handouts in real life hit home. No longer were they simply words in the articles and far removed from my daily life. But when I saw these poor people in person, the problems I read about became very real.

The least I could do was to amplify their struggles and heartaches through my reporting, and show the public the problems resulting from the pandemic, and encourage the community to help those less fortunate.

Before the coronavirus outbreak, Hong Kong had already experienced months of social unrest. A University of Hong Kong study found that around a third of adults had symptoms of post-traumatic stress disorder in 2019. And in 2020, with Covid-19, Hongkongers were experiencing an unprecedented level of mental health issues.

I was surprised to learn from the reverend that the people of Hong Kong had kept up their donations during these hard times. I had mistakenly thought that since events and gatherings, such as charity galas, were not allowed during the pandemic, that donations would have halted too. But despite the restrictions, many people wanted to help the poor and the donations kept pouring in.

I also spoke to a leader of a nonprofit network helping the poor, who said that because the pandemic had lasted for so long, many of the poor didn't see any hope.

'For a lot of people who are poor, they want to maintain their dignity,' she said. 'Even though they are poor, they still want to try and take care of themselves, try to make ends meet, even maybe only having one meal a day . . . But things are so tough now, they may not even have that one meal per day, so they have to come out and seek support.'

She introduced me to Cheuk, who lived in the neighbourhood for more than twenty years and used to drive a cab. Cheuk rented his cab and a place to stay from the car owner. But then they had a falling out, and Cheuk stopped driving for the owner. He also lost his place of abode. With no income, Cheuk became homeless five years ago.

When Cheuk and I first spoke on the phone, we got along immediately. Perhaps I reminded him of his daughter who was only a few years younger than myself.

He mentioned that he was not around much when she was growing up, so he felt that he owed her. Maybe that's why he patiently explained his situation to me and tried to help me to understand what had happened to him.

This was my first time interviewing a homeless person and learning about his day-to-day life. It was an eye-opener.

Cheuk told me that his biggest worry was that he didn't have a job and didn't have a place to live. If he could find a job then he wouldn't have to worry about his meals and a roof over his head.

He spent his days at the public library, going on the internet and applying for work. But during the worst days of the pandemic, the public libraries closed. Cheuk couldn't look for a job and he wandered the streets. I hadn't thought about how the closure of the government's public facilities would affect the underprivileged who depended on the services.

Usually at 7 p.m. or 8 p.m., Cheuk would go to a twenty-four-hour fast-food restaurant, and eat leftover French fries, chicken nuggets, and soda. And when many of the customers had left, he would find a bench in a quiet corner and catch a few hours of sleep. But on the worst days, dine-in services ended at 6 p.m. so Cheuk had to sleep outdoors.

While I was upset that restaurants had to close by six at night and I couldn't go out to dinner with my family nor friends, I was shocked that poor people literally lost a roof over their heads for weeks at a time.

At one point, his lower legs became infected, but the public shower facilities were closed so he couldn't clean the wounds properly, only making them worse. He showed me photos of his blistering, raw skin and I cringed. I learned that when a scab forms, the infection is starting to heal.

I was really shocked to hear Cheuk's story. I had struggled during the pandemic. My colleagues, family, and friends had struggled. But we lived in a bubble. Our struggles were nothing compared to what Cheuk had to go through. He couldn't go to the library anymore during the day. And he lost any chance he had to get out of his current predicament through finding a job. He didn't have a safe indoor place to sleep at night, instead he had to brave the elements. And his health got worse.

Luckily his story had a happy ending. He met a church group and it helped him find a job as a security guard, and he rented a room in a hostel.

But there are many more people like Cheuk in the city who fell on hard times, and lost their jobs. He is someone's father, brother, uncle, cousin, son, grandfather. And the pandemic made their lives so much worse. They need our kindness.

Now that Cheuk has turned his life around, I hope he and his daughter will reunite. He wants to be a bigger part of her life but also doesn't want to burden her.

On another day, I met a proud, middle-aged man, Ahmed, as he was about to start his overnight shift delivering produce. It was almost midnight as he started loading the light-goods truck with boxes of fruits and vegetables. He had to deliver the produce to the markets before they opened in the morning. Some boxes were as much as forty kilograms. He was afraid of getting injured, losing his job and not being able to provide for his family. He was afraid of becoming poor.

I admired Ahmed very much. As an immigrant, he was performing backbreaking work to make ends meet for his family.

He reminded me of my parents who emigrated from Hong Kong to the United States, and were often treated as outsiders. But their struggles in a foreign country were worth it for the promise of a better future for their children.

Ahmed was grateful to have found the delivery job. At the beginning of the pandemic, he barely earned enough to pay for rent, and had to borrow from his relatives to put food on the table.

Originally from Pakistan, Ahmed immigrated to Hong Kong as a teenager. He's lived in the city almost all his life and attended primary school. So he could read, write, and speak the local language, Cantonese.

My parents took English classes in the United States for years. They can read, write, and speak. But they don't speak perfect American English. Is that why they are still treated as outsiders? Or is it because of the colour of their hair and skin?

Many of Ahmed's friends and relatives were not as fortunate as he was. And those who were not literate in Cantonese were at a distinct disadvantage. Some of Ahmed's friends struggled to find work during the pandemic. He and other South Asians were considered ethnic minorities in Hong Kong, and were often discriminated against. And this was exacerbated during the pandemic.

For instance, my building management refused to allow the South Asian delivery men into the complex believing they spread Covid-19. But the same rules didn't apply to the Chinese delivery men.

And with rising anti-foreigner sentiment in Hong Kong, I felt lucky to blend in with the majority ethnic Chinese population even though I wasn't from the city. Ahmed and many of his family and friends bore the brunt of the increasing xenophobia.

Even my own family who had lived in the United States for nearly fifty years were being treated as outsiders with the rising anti-Asian hate during the pandemic. My mother was afraid of going to the Asian supermarkets because women like her had been robbed. I tried to encourage my family to carry pepper spray. I knew other elderly Asians were taking self-defense classes.

While they may never become an insider in their adopted homes, I hope my parents' dream, and Ahmed's dream, of making better lives for their children can help them overcome the obstacles and hatred from the pandemic.

When this report aired on television, it received an overwhelming response from the public. I received a message on social media from a man who said his wife cried while watching my report and that it was a big reality check. Another person on social media wanted to help Cheuk and direct him to food banks and find him housing. Several members of the public emailed the station wanting to buy a computer for Ling and provide a job for her mother, Mei.

The struggles of poor people during the pandemic were a universal theme at the time. These were the stories of security guards, street cleaners, and beggars who were our neighbours and part of our community. We would be so wrapped up in our own lives and our own struggles during the pandemic, myself included, that we would forget about those around us who might be suffering even more.

Meeting all these people and producing this news report reminded me of one of the fundamental reasons that I became a journalist: to give a voice to the voiceless. This assignment became a wake-up call for the public, but in many emotional ways, also for myself. Very few people in the world were untouched by the pandemic, but the poor, the marginalized, the invisible were much more affected. But my work could make them not so invisible after all.

Travel and Nature Writing in the Time of Covid-19

By Muna Noor

It's August 2021 and life has become divided into pre- and post-Covid existences.

Life pre-Covid was immediate and demanding. To cope, we took our pleasures often and whenever we could. We spent time with our friends and family crammed around the dinner table to eat and trade stories; some of us ran marathons or went to the gym; and when we craved a change of scene we escaped.

Budget airline, AirAsia's motto, Now Everyone Can Fly, captured the jet-fuel-paced zeitgeist. We flew to foreign places as often as our bosses and budgets would allow; we communed at art galleries, museums and music festivals; we shopped until we dropped; gathered on pink beaches and snowy peaks; and we fêted life with sunset cocktails from rooftop bars that overlooked yet another unfamiliar city.

Joining a workforce of fresh graduates as an eager-to-impress staff writer for a men's lifestyle magazine, I too was swept up in the tumultuousness of life, only to leave fulltime employment in 2014. I had burned out and faced a professional existential crisis. Digital publishing in Malaysia was in its difficult adolescent years. The technological advancements were thrilling but the constant pursuit of page views and engagement had become draining, and as often occurs to those in middle management, my role had morphed into one WIP meetings, conference calls and team huddles designed to extract as much money as possible from clients. I barely wrote or ideated in meaningful ways—my job did not spark joy—so I turned my back on the cushy media junkets, red carpet events and constant deadlines, and after some soul searching, embarked on a life of freelance writing, travelling on my own terms and advocating for nature and wildlife. In a nutshell, I became lonely, broke and content.

Pokok Kelapa, my travel blog, was started on a whim. The Malay word for coconut tree, it was named for the tree that reminds me of tropical holidays and provides Southeast Asians with an abundance of life's necessities, from food and drink to building and roofing materials. Pokok Kelapa filled a hole in my often-empty schedule—freelance writing consists of long periods of Netflix and nothingness followed by frantic periods of over extension—and became a record of my journeys, hiking sojourns and volunteer adventures for nature and wildlife NGOs.

I travelled extensively to small towns and through foreign countryside then, and as new flight routes opened up, I explored some of Southeast Asia most magical cities. I fulfilled my father's lifelong wishes to travel with him to Lake Toba in Sumatra to reconnect with my Batak roots, rode the old train from Bangkok to Kanchanaburi's 'River Kwai' to contemplate life, death and the futility of war; and in the remote frontier town of Berau in East Kalimantan I helped to construct a playground for rescued orangutans struggling to survive in forest landscapes threatened by logging, monoculture and mining. By doing something for the voiceless, I discovered my voice; and by connecting with nature, I learned to slow down and connect with people. Like the humble coconut tree from which it derives its name, Pokok Kelapa became a statement of utility. If it happened to ignite inspiration in whatever Google Search user haplessly came across it, that was a bonus. To my surprise, it gained an unlikely following as a hiking blog.

Due to my interests and flexible work situation, I was able to avoid the pitfalls of over-tourism on my sojourns, but as time wore on I became increasingly aware of problem. In Venice, locals decried the cruise ships that entered the city's fragile lagoon and emptied thousands of day trippers onto its already overwhelmed canals and passageway. In Barcelona an influx of tacky souvenir stores and chain restaurants had already irreparably transformed the character of many treasured parts of the city. I saw similar parallels in Penang and Malacca, Malaysia's UNESCO World Heritage site, where local residents and enterprise had been priced out of traditional neighbourhoods.

Even remote locations were not spared. Over the last decade, hiking has exploded as a pursuit in Malaysia. There are numerous groups catering to those with an interest in hiking, outdoor and adventure activities and they continue to grow: Hiking And Camping Around Malaysia (HACAM), a public Facebook group established in 2008, is the largest with over 3,60,000 members.

The virality of social media platforms, a power capable of drawing attention to places of interest, also threatened to overwhelm them. Instagram's power to drive hundreds, even thousands, of people a day to a beauty spot on the basis of a single popular image, represents the zenith of the negative aspects of mass tourism.

I could see the effects. Alarmingly, I was even contributing to the problem. Trails that were mostly deserted, even during the peak periods of weekends and holidays, became overrun, with some showing the hallmarks of overuse. Misled by social media images painting a simplistic picture of what summiting a mountain entails, the levels of fitness it requires and the equipment that is needed, there has been a corresponding rise in the numbers of underprepared hikers requiring rescue by the civil authorities. Though it was a wildly unpopular idea amongst the hiking fraternity at the time, I was warming to the notion of mandatory hiking permits, increased cost of entry and enforced carrying capacities.

And then, in 2018, the Flygskam movement happened. Emerging around the same time that Greta Thunberg began skipping school to lead the first climate strikes, *flygskam* is a Swedish term that means flight shame. The idea took hold more than a decade after environmentalist and author George Monbiot declared that 'The growth in aviation and the need to address climate change cannot be reconciled' in the book 'Heat'. Flygskam called on the wanderlust to give up or reduce their air travel. At the current rate of growth, commercial flying was predicted in 2020 to account for sixteen per cent of global carbon emissions by 2050.

This hit close to home. Kuala Lumpur, where I am based, is an international travel hub. Forests flamed, icecaps melted and polar bears starved. The world careened towards climate destruction and the imminent collapse of biodiversity and extinction. As a travel writer I recognized the role I played in this unfolding disaster. As an environmentally conscious one who needed to get paid, I wrestled with the ethical dilemma. My post-career crisis of meaning was nearing completion. In the daily churn of the bad news cycle and individual helplessness in the face of big industry apathy I knew I wasn't alone in wistfully dreaming of a planetary do-over.

As they say, be careful what you wish for . . . .

Just as the rest of the world was preparing to ring in 2020, a small team of female journalists from Hong Kong broadsheet South China Morning Post filed a report detailing the emergence of a 'mystery pneumonia' in Wuhan, China. Cases of the unknown viral disease had been linked to a seafood market that was later revealed to trade in exotic wildlife. Having written about the poaching crisis in Malaysia and the impact of animal trafficking on endangered species, news of the emergence of a new and potentially life-threatening zoonotic disease was as disconcerting as it was depressingly inevitable.

Within a fortnight, cases of SARS-CoV-2, later known as Covid-19, were detected in Southeast Asia, and by the end of January had made their own transcontinental journeys to the US and Europe. Safe, affordable long-distance air travel had transformed the world, turning it into a smaller, more highly connected place, and this deadly scourge was hitching a ride on its success.

As countries closed their borders, I joined the legion of travellers attempting to cancel travel arrangements and recoup costs. As a lifestyle writer, I'm trained to track a trend and predict new ones; it wasn't difficult to see where this was heading. When the Malaysian government announced its first Movement Control Order in March 2020, and permitted only essential businesses and services to operate, I had a full calendar and a number of assignments lined up, including stories for several inflight magazines. Overnight, these were put on hold.

As Covid-19 turned from a concerning outbreak into a global pandemic, stories were spiked and editors stopped answering emails. Amidst a decade of declining advertising revenues, publishing and publishers faced yet another existential crisis. To survive, editorial departments were restructured, staff laid off, budgets slashed, and, consequently, freelance work dried up.

Travel restrictions reduced the frequency of flights, grounding some air carriers completely. The Flygskam movement suddenly seemed superfluous, overtaken by realities on the ground. The aviation industry became one of the hardest hit sectors and I was left wondering not so much whether in-flight magazines will resume publication once restrictions are lifted, but whether there will be an industry to publish them for.

Like workers in many sectors around the world, freelance travel writers re-invented themselves in order to stay relevant and gainfully employed, Instead of writing long form essays about exotic locales and short punchy listicles screaming places to visit before you die, we were now rolling with the news cycle, covering topics such as how to get holiday refunds, and cataloguing the latest hotel closures, peppered with hopeful stories about travel bubbles and what travel would look like when it finally resumed.

I did that for a turn; relaying the opening and closure announcements of public and national parks and state forests, but the constantly changing safety operating procedures made it a dissatisfying job. With hiking halted in Malaysia during its most stringent movement restrictions, tired trails were bouncing back even as my site's traffic took a dive off a steep cliff. The flagging numbers were discouraging, but not unexpected.

Within the toolkit of any decent staff writer or editor is the ability to conceive a story from multiple angles or recast it in different forms; I could rewrite old stories and had a backlog of stories to clear, but they were neither timely nor relevant (key deciders in whether a story is deemed newsworthy) and publishing them seemed disingenuous. It was impossible to tell whether that historic small-town ice cream shop or traditional crafts store would still be there after the pandemic. Plus, with more pressing concerns on everyone's minds, there was a lack of public appetite for travel stories.

I was used to being outdoors, in nature. Being indoors for prolonged periods affected my mental state. Urged to stay inside, I was no longer able to enjoy the horizon, which is obscured by link houses to the sides, front and back of my own home. I felt robbed of much needed perspective, literally and figuratively. For months I suffered from writer's block.

Yet there were opportunities. Being confined gave me a chance to upskill and widen my talents. That began with a short but necessary course on Imposter Syndrome. That feeling has plagued me as a freelance writer: the rejected pitches, the feeling of being on the periphery of the conversation, the pressure to present yourself as a well-read expert on the given topic, but ultimately knowing barely enough to frame the argument. It formed a perfect storm of debilitating self-doubt. The course helped. I remain a work in progress but with my confidence, if not restored, then at least resurgent, other courses and workshops on career boosting topics followed.

Interest groups, NGOs and academics took to virtual technologies to host lectures, talks and chair discussions to share their work during global lockdowns. The growing prevalence of video streaming tools like Facebook Live, Zoom and as of late Clubhouse provided direct access to experts in numerous fields. It was like discovering treasure, and I greedily grabbed it up; I gathered information, squirreled away story leads and saved contact details.

I learned to lean in, to look closer and find value in the hyperlocal. Putrajaya, where I live, is both a city and a state, less than 50 square kilometres in size. Used to chasing mountains and escaping to far flung destinations, I began to write about neighbourhood parks and local urban trails. When the often-fluid government restrictions on movement permitted, I would venture into often forgotten and overlooked locales slightly further afield.

It was painful to recognize that, despite my best efforts, I continued to add to the problems that the travel industry creates. But the time spent away from the things that mattered most to me gave me the mental space to gain some much-needed perspective: to acknowledge that I had to be a part of the solution and to figure out the best way to contribute.

The pandemic showed the ugly cracks in a broken system. In the unsustainable pursuit of 'growth at all costs' we had come to value the wrong things at the expense of the right ones: money and spectacle over people, time and nature. We rediscovered the value and importance of under-appreciated professions like medical personnel, teachers, cleaners and scientists.

As emissions dropped, skies and waterways cleared. With minimal human disturbance, nature ventured into spaces previously occupied by human activities. Our systemic abuse and blatant disrespect of nature may have led to the onset of Covid-19 (and other zoonotic viruses), but nature's response as the machinery of human existence grinds to a halt demonstrated that it's not too late, and that change is possible. If we are to continue to have a world that is worth exploring, those changes will need to be systemic and far-sighted, and the travel sector is no exception. Travel may be a luxury and a privilege, but tourism is not only critical for the economy of many countries, it can be a force for good, capable of supporting industries, creating jobs, providing a livelihood for marginalized communities and funding critical conservation projects.

In September 2020, in his first post during a short but spectacular run on Instagram, the celebrated environmentalist and broadcast journalist Sir David Attenborough described saving the planet as a 'communications challenge'. As members of the Fourth Estate, travel and nature writers, me among them, have an opportunity to link growing environmental awareness to a rise in sustainable, community-focused travel and hold stakeholders accountable for seeing this through.

To that end, Pokok Kelapa will continue to champion off-kilter destinations, slow travel and volunteering opportunities that make real and lasting impact on nature and communities that rely on it—and, yes—flying only when necessary.

When Malaysia briefly loosened its movement restrictions in mid-2020 there was a surge in interest in activities like hiking and cycling. Visitors to Pokok Kelapa doubled overnight. Would these would-be travellers be part of the problem or the solution? As an advocacy journalist capable of shaping public opinion with fair and accurate reporting, to empower the individual, amplifying a single voice and spurring collective action, I viewed this growth spurt as an opportunity to recruit an army of potential environmental protectors. Eloquently captured in the Malay proverb *Tak kenal, maka tak cinta* which translates as 'to know, is to love', this appeal to understanding and appreciation has the transformative power to turn the public need to access nature and outdoor experiences into a desire to protect these spaces when imperilled.

As an active member of the hiking and nature communities I write about, I've also decided to serve it offline as well as on. I helped to cut my first community trail. I extended the reach of my blog, and my own limited influence, to organize my first beach clean-up during a period of low infection rates and looser movement controls.

(At time of writing) I'm still confined to the city-state I live in, and Covid-19 cases continue to spike nationally even as vaccination numbers are rising. On bad days, the pessimist in me envisions an eternal lockdown, a future of four walls and the collapse of society. History and travel are a reminder that all empires eventually fall. I've seen it first-hand in the ancient ruins and former colonial outposts I've travelled to; and this year we've watched California and Southern Europe burn, and the Gulf of Mexico catch fire.

On good days, I'm reminded that the means to solve our pressing problems is within our collective capabilities. The international cooperation that has helped us to face this contagion. The determination to produce viable vaccines in the shortest possible time and the collective effort needed to quell mistruths and disinformation. Not to mention the personal journey required to change many of us from individuals into contributing members of supportive communities.

The world's nations are yet to throw open their borders to global tourism but there are signs of recovery, and a gradual and limited restoration of regional and local travel links offers a glimmer of hope. I'm fortunate that my small circle and I are now fully vaccinated. The side effects include restrained optimism and future planning. With proper care, this recovery could create a better world and a more meaningful approach to tourism.

A Walkthrough the Downfall of MO1

By Ushar Daniele

It was hard to think that any actual outcome of this particular conviction would emerge.

Years of disappointments, rulings overturned with the guilty walking free in Malaysia can of course lead one to be jaded and sceptical after almost ten years being a journalist telling stories on the ground.

Hours, days, months and even years spent covering one of the largest cases of kleptocracy had finally come to an end, so I thought.

The afternoon of 3 July 2018 was not like any other and I was an eager independent journalist who had just departed a local newspaper—seeking for stories to file and it was all made possible as a freelancer because I had begun producing television content for a popular American news outlet as well as for a Middle Eastern network.

Somewhere mid-afternoon of the day, a text message arrived on my phone from a close friend and journalist, Hadi Azmi which said: 'Words from higher up says MO1 is being arrested'.

I sat down, trying to comprehend the piece of information and that somehow felt like justice on its own.

A former prime minister was being arrested and it was not going to be a private affair.

The Malaysian press core was ruthless and how could you not be when you're thrown deep into a story that was so vile, it would make your stomach churn.

While court coverage wasn't as sensational as a murder deep in the forest, emotions ran deep with intense lines of questioning by public prosecutors and heated rebuttals by criminal lawyers.

All I could think of was that this man could possibly one day be seen, photographed and filmed wearing a prison uniform.

The former premier, or MO1, a moniker given by the United States Department of Justice for successfully being a key personality in one of the largest cases of kleptocracy in the world.

This MO1 was not just a man on the street as he come from an elite line of leadership bloodline.

His father was the second Prime Minister of Malaysia—it was easy to figure out the lavish life he had lived.

It becomes even more bizarre knowing that this MO1 pocketed RM2.6 billion and in 2017, his intense web of denial and lies began unravelling.

The arrest came at a historical time in Malaysia's timeline.

After 60 years of deteriorating governance, its ruling party fell and MO1's downfall came swiftly.

Knowing the urgency of the story—I had to alert the bosses in Hong Kong.

Every second in the journalism world was a second you could not afford to lose as a story such as this could develop into something bigger at any given time.

I knew I would bump into the who's who of the industry and it was time to pack up to head out to Putrajaya, the administrative capital of Malaysia.

Putrajaya was also the headquarters for Malaysia Anti Corruption Commission and that was where MO1 would be held.

Reading bits of information that trickles in every ten minutes was enough to drive an anxious reporter into a frenzy.

I, for one, was in the comforts of my home, working remotely when I received the news.

With no time to spare, I changed into something more 'journalist' and drove to Putrajaya in autopilot mode and while driving there, the only thought I had was this really happening?

Was the former Prime Minister of Malaysia, who vehemently denied any wrongdoings or idea of the embezzlement, really getting arrested?

This would be a far-fetched idea if the former governing coalition party was still in power.

MO1 gripped onto power for over eight years, surviving two terms in government as the scandal grew bigger and bigger, headlining international media day after day.

The attention his 'associate' who we shall call Mr J had received in the media was enough to make anyone sick.

Champagne bottles, diamonds, lavish spending, supermodels and celebrities.

Those words strung together was enough to explain the person Mr J had presented himself as.

Meanwhile, in Malaysia, critics of MO1 during his premiership faced persecution.

It was 2009 when it all started and to-date, it held the rank of the largest financial scandal in the world.

MO1 wasn't in the golden circle with his money just sitting by himself for he had friends who enabled the siphoning.

Mr J was known throughout the globe for his close links to the state fund and yet, he remains a fugitive till today.

When MO1 formed the state fund, it had a goal and it was to elevate the nation's economy.

When researching bits of the story for background and understanding of the investment flows, a throbbing headache was imminent.

First, well of course, the investment fund wasn't making any money but instead, it amassed US$12 billion in debts.

Being a journalist in Malaysia—corruption was nothing new really. It was tea-time talk at most but when MO1's personal piggy bank started to alert authorities, it became something you'd have to tread carefully when reporting it.

The cherry on top of the breaking news day was the announcement by the United States Department of Justice.

The newsroom was havoc—reporters and editors had their eyes glued onto the television to watch the announcement and with every minute it, you could see eyebrows raising every so frequently.

I can say the sentiment across the nation was the same—what the hell is happening and how did this happen?

Between 2009 and 2014, more than US$4.5 billion was embezzled from the funds and it found its way to various shell accounts before conveniently landing itself in the hands of these corrupt officials.

A brief explainer of the soiree, the state fund was incepted in July 2009 but no one had an idea of what was really happening with the state fund.

It was strange though, over the years of covering multiple new investments made by the sovereign fund, there was never really any updates on its profits.

I started out my career in journalism as a rookie reporter in 2013 and by the time my editors trusted me with a big story such as the sovereign state fund—it was already falling apart.

Between 2009 and 2012, MO1 and his friends including Mr J raised billions of dollars under the pretext of suitable investments that could not only attract foreign direct investments but also boost its domestic economy, so they say.

In 2013, however, the walls came crumbling down for MO1 and those involved.

Reporting on how a Malaysian state fund was involved in a major Hollywood production was bizarre, even as a junior reporter.

It was at a time where the people of Malaysia were slowly feeling the pinch of the poor economy.

Prices of goods were rising, the cost of living was rising and the unemployment rate was growing so it was only normal to hear grouses from the grassroots that times were tough.

The US$100 million Hollywood feature film struck the public in particular because it was produced by a company that was linked to MO1's stepson and a close confidant of Mr J.

Their game of 'siphon the money' came to light in 2015 when the state fund missed a loan payment and it was for US$550 million.

Of course, the talk of the town was how and why did the sovereign state fund, under the tutelage of the Prime Minister, miss a loan payment?

The usual investigation was launched in Malaysia and while it was difficult to report on it locally but internationally, the media exposed MO1 and his doings.

What broke the camel's back was when the world found out US$700 million, allegedly from the state fund had made its way into his personal bank account.

It was a busy few months after that came to light because it was when probes were launched against MO1, and he, who was still the prime minister at the time, shuffled his cards and cabinet.

The Attorney-General was booted and a new one conveniently swooped in to replace him—taking the lead of the fund's investigations.

He was cleared of all allegations and after reading and attending every press conference and statement from the investigations, as a reporter, you cannot help but question whether this man would ever be held responsible for siphoning huge sums of money from a fund that was meant for the people.

It was hard going into flooded areas and seeing people lose their homes and everything they own while you watch how MO1 and his family jet set across the world, dressed up in the finest silks and with expensive jewellery on display.

The investigations of course found MO1 not guilty of siphoning the money, maintaining innocence that it was a donation by the Kingdom of Saudi Arabia.

Pretty hard to escape from any form of scepticism really, how conveniently MO1 could return US$620 million and the case was closed.

The light at the tunnel came in the form of the United States Department of Justice (DoJ).

Their crackdown on the embezzlement saw civil suits filed for seizures of assets that were allegedly purchased with funds from the state fund.

MO1 had nowhere to run and nowhere to go when the DoJ revealed that US$4.5 billion had been siphoned from the state fund and a criminal probe was launched against MO1.

Headlines on local newspapers read 'kleptocracy at its worst' and in the coming weeks, reporters and editors were on the heel of everyone involved in the state fund for an exclusive story.

If I was MO1, I would hate May 2018 for the rest of my life because it was the month of my downfall.

MO1 and his party lost the 13th General Election and it was a step forward in democracy after sixty years of the same ruling government that had multiple tactics and manoeuvres to stay in power.

Stripped of his powers, there was nowhere to escape for MO1 and his family.

The former premier and his family were known to live a lavish life and what shocked the country and world was when police raided residences belonging to MO1, the authorities found luxury goods including jewellery, handbags and cash amounting up to US$275 million.

They were barred from leaving the country and for many of us covering the developing story—it was checkmate.

An air of relief came when he lost the election because we got to divulge the wrongdoings of a man who claimed innocence for many years.

We rushed to court the next day to watch MO1 claim trial for four charges laid against him.

The Kuala Lumpur High Court was packed to the brim with lawyers, reporters, camera crews and ultimately, MO1's hoard of supporters who stormed the corridors of the court compounds.

MO1 pleaded not guilty to three counts of criminal breach of trust and one count of abuse of power in connection with the state funds and brought with him a seven-man defence led by senior lawyers.

More corruption charges were laid against him the following year and MO1, the former prime minister and the son of the second prime minister of Malaysia saw forty-two criminal charges brought against him.

In two years, current affairs journalists like myself went in and out of the court compound, saying hello and goodbye to court officials almost every day.

MO1 was found guilty of seven charges on 28 July 2020 by the Malaysian High Court and sighs of relief were heard all around when the judge meted the sentence.

The days leading up to MO1's verdict and sentencing were intense.

We didn't know what to expect because it was pretty hard to gauge whether a politician like MO1 would and could be sentenced to imprisonment.

We've never had a former prime minister thrown into jail because it wasn't something the Malaysian judiciary did.

Having spent many days planning coverage for the big day, both for television and print, it was really taking a toll on a lot of us.

The sentencing came in the midst of a pandemic where strict rules were imposed, entrances were barred, masks were compulsory and seats were limited — it was a battleground and your peers were your allies.

It was a common thing in a media coverage lineup that the newswires were given the priority and then the mainstream press reporters.

Lined up in a row are the television cameras waiting to film every moment of the accused and his defence team and from afar, you would hear cameras clicking and its blinding flash capturing every moment in the court compound.

It was an early day for most of us and not exaggerating but arriving at the court compound at 6.30 a.m. was already considered late.

It has been months since many of us left our homes for assignments after the pandemic lockdowns came into effect and we knew that MO1 would have his usual supporters showing up in hordes at the courthouse.

We had to go through layers of police lines while trying to maintain distance from other lawyers and court visitors but patience was growing thin.

More supporters began showing up in the vicinity and journalist and cameraman who were huddled up were starting to worry if they would break barriers to show their support.

Nothing like that happened but being a journalist on location, any action is a good action because that means breaking news.

I was stationed in the video-link room.

The videolink room was a special live viewing feed from the courtroom that allowed more journalists to cover the case while maintaining social distancing because of the pandemic.

There were about fifty of us in a fish tank-like room in the basement of the court complex where many gathered and peeped through the clear glass hoping to hear or watch what transpired in the courtroom as MO1 faced the judge.

For twelve hours, we sat in the glass tank, watching a thirty-two-inch television waiting for a verdict to be read and a sentence to be meted.

When I joined journalism in 2013, MO1 was a prime minister that was known for two things, his wife, who called herself the 'First Lady of Malaysia', a title that does not exist in Malaysia and the state fund.

Working with a mainstream newspaper made it harder to report on the sovereign wealth fund as well because editors had to keep their bosses happy by only running positive propaganda stories about MO1.

It wasn't easy because my former boss at the time was friends with MO1 and he was even rumoured to show up at the office one day.

Now that I was working independently and there were no lackeys to give orders—it was a breath of fresh air.

It was time Malaysia and the world knew that MO1 was not the man he claimed to be and it was a privilege to be in the middle of it all to tell the story.

Those who didn't really understand the judiciary system continued to defend MO1's innocence but the day had come for him to face the music.

It was a long day—we were sitting in the room in the basement of the courthouse for twelve-hours. We waited for hours to go by as the court read hundreds of pages prepared by the prosecution after the two-year court proceeding.

When the time came for the verdict to be delivered, you could sense a changing vibe of the room when suddenly you could only hear the voice of the judge.

I heard gasps from the reporters sitting in front of me when the judge said, 'You are found guilty of seven charges' and trust me, it was a gasp of relief.

There was finally conviction for one of the largest cases of embezzlement ever to be executed by a head of state.

Malaysia was on the map for many things and MO1's state fund involvement Hollywood broke the Pandora's Box of all things corrupted.

The experience covering MO1's involvement in the scandal was definitely one of a kind.

In the early days when I was with the newspaper, we had to someway practise self censorship because either way, the bits that were rather unpleasant but true would be omitted from the report.

After years of following, reporting, writing and even talking about the crooks involved in the state fund, it was truly something watching someone like MO1 face imprisonment.

He still walks around as I write this, his team of lawyers were granted a stay pending appeal which allows MO1 to attend parliament and pretty much do whatever he wants except for leaving the country.

He attends parliament, he says whatever he wants on social media but truth to be told some of his postings are terribly funny.

The takeaway from his conviction was that no matter how abused you think the system may be, justice would prevail no matter what.

Was the years running back and forth to court to cover the case worth it?

Absolutely because I wouldn't trade it for anything else.

Inspirations from a Mistress
of Death

By Sher Maine Wong

I had never met a funeral director before. I never had to deal with death on a personal level.

But when a book publisher asked if I would like to ghost-write an autobiography of a funeral director in Singapore in 2015, I leapt at the chance. It would allow me to break through bone-dry freelance writing jobs which dealt with the likes of corporate achievements and technology transformations, and dive deep into what I really wanted to learn about: Death in Singapore.

Because for me that's why writing is a dream job. I get paid to satisfy my curiosity.

Apparently not many writers wanted to take on the job because in Asia, death is a topic to be avoided. '*Pantang*', they call it, Malay for taboo. Growing up in a fairly traditional Chinese household, my father would shout at me—'*Choi*! *Choi*! Don't say!' - if I were to even mention the word '*sei*', which is Cantonese for death.

But the thing about death is, everybody dies. I will die. And education has taught me that if there is any fear, the best way to overcome it is with knowledge.

The first time I met Angjolie—or AJ as I think of her—at the office of the book publisher so I could pitch myself as her writer, I was stunned.

Of course, I had done my online research. I knew the funeral director was a woman, that she was young—at least younger than I was—and that she looked suitably professional in her photos.

Face-to-face, AJ was far more saturated in appearance, personality and impact. In black high heels which announced her arrival to the publisher's office in staccato, she waltzed in in a black sleeveless peplum dress, one which I would learn later was part of a series of smart black dresses she kept on hand, suitable for wakes and funerals. Long jet-black hair, bright red lipstick, tanned skin and blood-red nails—always the blood-red nails—completed the look of the funeral director who really did not look like one.

Starting with the firm, warm handshake, which I associate with confidence and openness in people I meet for the first time, we got on like a house on fire because there was mutual trust and respect, and she was strong without being difficult. She remains one of the few clients who accepted my fee, which was not unreasonable, without question. I knew then she would not treat me like a paid minion but as a professional who knew writing better than she did. That would make it a fulfilling, enjoyable project which I would pour my heart into.

I would find out later that alongside funeral directing, her passion was salsa dancing, and her social media feed was filled with photos of her sunning by the beach in a bikini, travelling to far-off places, hanging out with friends who looked like they were from all over the world. 'Live life to the fullest,' she would tell me later.

In Singapore's tired, outdated funeral industry, one which had been dominated by middle-aged or elderly men with little education and whose lack of work choices showed in their lackadaisical T-shirt attire and chronic smoking of cigarettes while on the job, AJ was the rare young woman who stood out like a rising sun.

I got the job. Working on the book took one and a half years. For several months during the interview process, one morning each week, I would head to her walk-up apartment in the quaint Tiong Bahru area of Singapore. She would serve me English teas like Earl Grey or Chamomile in a glass mug, I would settle down to my laptop, press record on my mobile phone, and while the fan whirred sluggishly overhead and the birds chirped, I opened the window to her world.

While she was a rare woman in the male-dominated industry, I learnt that she was actually of funeral pedigree.

Her father was a giant in Singapore's funeral industry. In the face of land-scarce Singapore's push toward cremation rather than burial in the sixties and seventies, he was the one who started producing lighter caskets which burnt more easily, adorned with Buddhist motifs like lotus flowers so that the majority Chinese population would embrace cremation. Her housewife mother, when her father died in 2004, took over the reins of the business. Her sister became an embalmer.

When she told me that sister ended up marrying another funeral director, and that probably half of Singapore's funeral industry attended the dinner, I laughed when she told me how the management of the hotel where the wedding dinner took place complained at the hordes of funeral workers who were chain-smoking in the toilets.

Still, she was on a path which led away from funerals. AJ majored in psychology and economics at the university, and was a management trainee in a logistics company. Her mother did not want another daughter to enter the funeral industry. While it is one which is recession-proof, it is a 24/7 enterprise involving dead bodies and being discriminated against, especially in an Asian society.

When her mother married a funeral director, all her friends shunned her, for they feared that bad things would happen to them by associating with a woman whose husband dealt with death. When the company wanted to renovate the funeral parlour premises, interior designers and contractors did not want to do the job, and the only quotation which was eventually received was sky-high—as if a premium had been charged for having to do a *pantang* job.

But the choice was taken out of AJ's hands when her father, also a gambler, died, leaving six-figure debts behind. Not only did she step in to first support her mother, she later branched out on her own to start her own funeral company because she had a very clear idea of the kind of 'next-level' funerals she wanted to run. It would offer a higher level of service—with wait staff in suits serving visitors drinks, or sheltering them from the rain with corporate umbrellas—and more importantly, each funeral would be a bespoke event celebrating the life of the deceased.

Beyond our interviews, what I craved was being able to see, hear, smell, touch, experience. 'Are you sure?' she said, when I said I wanted to observe an embalming procedure, attend one of the funerals she organized, follow her on a day on the job. 'Yes of course,' I said. 'How can I write otherwise?'

I visited her office, one in a cluster of funeral parlours located in an out-of-the-way Geylang industrial estate alongside building and engineering companies, and learnt that most funeral companies are relegated to such sites because people do not like having one near their homes. I sat in at a wake, and was told for the first time that the red string which was placed on the table was actually for me to take and throw away once I left, to protect myself from malicious spirits.

Of all the experiences I had, it was a session to clean and prepare a body which proved most intense and poignant. I did not know what to expect, beyond thinking that I would have to have a strong stomach. The preparations to enter the room reinforced that perception, as I had to put on a special pair of boots and personal protective equipment including a gown, long gloves and a surgical face mask, and this was pre-Covid. Clearly, I would be in an environment where my safety might be at risk.

But to my surprise, the session with the deceased elderly gentleman on the table, who was covered with a white cloth most of the time, was dignified, even moving. From first cutting off the white twine which tied his big toes together—to prevent splaying of the feet during transportation from the morgue, AJ and her staff proceeded to gently wash him with a hand-held shower. Her explanation, and it was one which had never occurred to me, was that in many cases, terminally-ill patients who spend months in the hospital or hospice before they die might not have enjoyed a bath for months. Using sutures and other special devices, they closed the gentleman's eyes and mouth, before applying restorative make-up and referring to photographs to style his hair based on how he had worn it in life.

The session never felt clinical or detached. What made it moving was not only that they treated him gently and with care throughout, always ensuring that dignity was maintained, they also spoke to him— 'Uncle, we are going to comb your hair now so that you can look your best for your family'. AJ, who says she has never had a hint of a ghostly encounter, told me, 'To me, these are Uncles and Aunties who I am preparing for their last journey in life. Speaking to them is also my way of showing respect to them.'

Among all the jobs I have undertaken in my freelance writing career, working on AJ's book was probably the one which touched my personal life the most, because it forced me to reflect on my own life and how I wanted to live it.

I did not think of death as taboo to start out with. But as I worked with her, I decided to start conversations with my parents on the kind of funerals they wanted. Perhaps age had made them mellow, but they were surprisingly open, and shared with me that my Cantonese grandmother had paid for and bought her own set of funeral clothes or *shouyi* (寿衣), all ready to be worn, years before she died in her early 90s. My parents had made no such preparations, and I have not managed to advance the conversation beyond 'have you made your wills?' and 'how do you want your ashes to be kept?' On that note, to their original assertion that they wanted sea burials, I shared with them that their ashes can nourish a growing plant and be turned into a diamond I can wear. Their verdict is still out.

Suicide was another topic which AJ could never stop talking about, and it made me reflect on the lonely or toxic people around me, who had somehow alienated their family and friends, and whether they ever felt suicidal.

For AJ, having attended to 'jumpers'—people who choose to jump off one of the many high-rise buildings in Singapore, those who hang themselves, and others who chose to end their lives in a variety of ways, each one stabbed her heart.

'What would make someone choose to end their own lives?' she would mutter, again and again, with furrowed brow, after she described every harrowing funeral which she had to organize with family members who were still reeling from grief. 'If they had special powers to fast-forward and see their grieving family members, would they still do it?'

Suicide seems a rising trend in Asia. There is school and economic pressure which exerts a devastating toll on mental health, and then now there is the pandemic, which has reportedly driven suicide numbers.

In Thailand, which apparently has the highest suicide rate in Asia, numbers went up by twenty-two per cent in the first six months of 2020 compared to the same period in 2019.

In all the stories she told, what stood out was how no one could tell, that loved ones or friends were going to kill themselves. One case which weighed heavily on her heart, was a young woman who had used AJ's company's services to pre-plan her own funeral—from music, artworks to be displayed, attire she would wear, to style of make-up—and paid for it. It is advanced planning, meant to relieve family members from the stress and hassle of having to make all these decisions while grieving. What AJ never expected, was that shortly after making payment, her client actually killed herself. She found out later that it was likely due to the client's husband having an affair, and her pre-planning was an intentional prelude to the end. 'Why didn't we see it?' she murmured.

I did not want to be someone who would exclaim in horror after the fact, at how I had no idea a friend or someone dear to me had suicidal thoughts, at how I had not cared enough to help. It made me more intentional in meeting up with people I cared about, and even some I didn't really care for, just to provide a listening ear, maybe bring some joy to their lives.

Then there is the whole spiel about how we have only one life to live. Cliched, perhaps, but death is the soil from which cliches spring to life and AJ utters plenty, all backed up with her work experience: Live with no regrets, leave with no regrets. Don't add days to your life, add life to your days. A funeral is not a day in a lifetime, it is a lifetime in a day.

She told me many stories, about someone who dropped dead while eating chicken rice, a best friend who was hit by a cement mixer, about dressing and caring for the body of a young Singaporean celebrity who died in a military exercise from a mistake which spanned several seconds.

Indeed, as a newspaper journalist, one of my starkest assignments was when I, aged twenty-five then, was sent to Taiwan in 2000 to cover the crash of Singapore Airlines flight 006. It never took off and bumped into a barrier as it traversed the runway, killing eighty-one of 179 people onboard. I will never forget casting my eyes on a photograph of a woman's blackened burnt legs in a Taiwanese hospital as her child and husband, who understandably refused to speak to the media, wept nearby. She died a few days later.

When I came back to the office, I was offered psychological counselling. News journalists are never far from death. I did not take it up the offer as I quickly got busy or distracted, with other things. But working with AJ made me, also perhaps I was older, to consider death on a more serious and deeper level. Life is short. And in the process of writing the book, I realized I wanted to live mine authentically without having to pretend or lie to anyone. It meant making certain difficult and major life choices, which up till now, I do not regret.

It meant thinking about and working through four phrases which she says people typically only say—too late—to a dead person: 'I'm sorry. Please forgive me. I thank you. I love you.' Simple expressions which are so difficult to utter, to the living, which I hope to work through, sometimes not verbally but by action. For instance, it is far easier for me—maybe because I was raised in a Chinese household where displays of emotion are frowned upon—to show my parents I love them by regularly treating them to meals and chatting with them about 'safe' topics like how they hardly had any side-effects from their Covid-19 jabs, than to tell them 'I love you'.

It meant that I wanted to define my life, not with possessions or even with memorable experiences, but with values like kindness, generosity and an open heart, which people at my funeral would ideally verbalize in their eulogies.

And then, when it all leads up to what AJ calls my life graduation ceremony, I know that there would be truly something to celebrate at my funeral.

Jungle Camps and Mass Graves

By Amy Sawitta Lefevre

There were dozens of them in the room and their eyes stared back. Some were visibly exhausted and others had their heads bowed in prayer. We drove from the airport in Phuket through winding roads hugged by rich jungle to a Thai government shelter in Phang Nga province. Sitting at our news bureau in Bangkok, my colleagues and I had received a tip off that a group of men were found wandering near mangrove forests, half-starved and surviving off of leaves. Were they from Myanmar? Bangladesh? Malaysia? How did they end up here?

By that point, I'd been a reporter for nearly five years, nearly three of them with Reuters - the venerable news agency that I will always refer to as the ultimate finishing school for wire journalism. Going from a news reader at a local television station in Bangkok to one of the finest news agencies in the world had catapulted me into the world of hard news but although I'd covered deadly floods in Thailand in 2011, political protests in Bangkok and a coup d'état that May (2014) I still didn't feel like I'd covered *that* story—the one that defines a reporter's career.

Just a few months earlier, an interview that our team had planned with then Thai Prime Minister Yingluck Shinawatra was cut short abruptly as her aides hurriedly told us that the military compound, we were in was surrounded by anti-government protests and the prime minister had to make a quick exit. We piled into the company car at a military base north of Bangkok, our cameraman nearly forgetting to take us with him in his haste , and made a mad dash for the nearest, safe exit while rumours swirled that the prime minister had escaped by helicopter. Following months of protracted political protests, Yingluck was eventually ousted.

Loathe her or like her, I had been able to observe Yingluck at a distance for several years and watched with horror how the fact that she was a female made her fair game for a host of public insults—her male adversaries, even the supposedly educated ones, called her 'barbie' or, worse, 'stupid bitch'. To some, the Thai coup of 2014 came as a relief and a welcome pause from the yellow shirt/red shirt divide that had plagued Thailand since Yingluck's brother, controversial Thai Prime Minister Thaksin Shinawatra, was ousted.

That wasn't to be my most difficult reporting of 2014. By October, I was at the shelter in Phang Nga, Southern Thailand—a location known outside of Thailand for its beaches and some hedonistic parties where people would flock to dance semi naked. Beyond the tourist brochures and postcard scenes, however, something sinister was happening.

The terms 'human trafficking', 'human smuggling' and 'jungle camps' were starting to become a regular part of the news cycle and, tellingly, even local news reporters were beginning to report the story that was essentially critical of their government and the authorities because of their inept response the mounting trafficking crisis. Thailand knew it faced a problem and that it was facing criticism to tackle it. Thailand was placed on Tier 3 of the US State Department's Trafficking in Persons (TIP) report—a rating reserved for countries with the worst human-trafficking records. In-depth reports by my colleagues the previous year had shown that thousands of Rohingya Muslims were being trafficked and sometimes held against their will in brutal trafficking camps along the Thai-Malaysia border.

Back at the shelter in Takua Pa, I had taken a trusted Rohingya interpreter along assuming that these people had arrived, like so many before them, from Myanmar. He began speaking to them and then turned to me: *'These people don't speak Rohingya. I don't understand them.' 'Are you sure?',* was my response. *'Yes, and they don't speak Burmese either.'* Over several hours, and with the help of an interpreter loaned from the local authorities, I tried to piece together their stories before we would be shut off from interview access to them by the International Organization for Migration. That report, which I refer to as the 'eating leaves' story because the trafficking victims had survived on leaves, was the first of what was to become my personal and professional series and multi-year, all-consuming involvement in reporting human trafficking stories and, eventually, facing some of the perpetrators of these crimes.

I had never in my reporting career seen such a jarring scene. Rows upon rows of men who were evidently not Thai were sitting in the government shelter. I learned that the men in Takua Pa were mostly from Teknaf in Bangladesh and the story of how they got there played in my head long after we left Phang Na, not least because the peculiarity of their journey was to lead to bigger investigations around journeys that evoked the horrors of the Atlantic slave trade. The men told me stories about being blindfolded with their hands tied. Some were drugged, others were conscious when they were forced onto small boats that took them to ships where they survived on scraps of food for weeks and where they were forced to squat for days at a time. According to survivors, men who died aboard those boats were sometimes thrown to the fish, women raped by their captors on the boat while the rest of those aboard the prison boat were powerless to help. I remember it affected me deeply and I had long conversations with Andrew, my mentor at the time, about the encounter that day. It was a pivotal moment that gave purpose to my journalism journey and brought about a very personal realization that this was why I wanted to do journalism—to shine a light on these horrors.

That night, after a long day of interviews, my team and I, the photographer, a legendary cameraman and our intrepid interpreter piled in our rental car while the driver sped to Phuket airport. As the rain lashed down and the driver took corners at 120 km an hour to try to get us to the airport on time, I could only think of two things and mumbled both as I do when flashes of religiousness take hold of me: *Please don't let me die today and please let me report more of these stories.* I couldn't believe what we had landed on. The Special Report my colleague Andrew and I published (*Traffickers use abductions, prison ships to feed Asian slave trade)* was the first of many reports about the subject in the second half of the year.

What does it take to become a *proper* journalist, I wondered? I had been warned by a more seasoned colleague that the news wires could trap you at your desk and in the newsroom, receiving news from stringers in the field (the real hard workers) while you tried to piece together a story elegantly. I made it my mission after several warnings and much encouragement from him to get out. Anywhere. Protest? Send me. A bomb blast? I'll run there. The behaviour became akin to that of an adrenaline junkie. Nearly a year later, in May 2015, I followed these people who had been trafficked to the end of their journey and made a trek to see what was possibly one of the hallmarks of my young career.

Just a few hundred metres from Thailand's border with Malaysia in the province of Songkhla volunteers, the world's press, Thai reporters, medics and military officials had gathered to set out for the day. We waited for what felt like hours and set out in convoys of news trucks, hired cars, ambulances and military vehicles. It was meant to be a spectacle. Thailand was under pressure to show the world her progress in combatting human trafficking and we were going to be taken, albeit in a very controlled fashion, finally, to see the jungle camps where human trafficking victims, many of them from Myanmar, had been held. So many had reported on these camps and witnesses had given approximate locations and coordinates, but few had seen them.

Our photographer assigned to the day, a veteran and accoladed giant in his field, moaning for most of the trek up what was a hill but felt like a mountain. He had seen so much more in his time covering wars and natural disasters but for me it would be the first time I would see a human body. I dreaded what we would find and thought of the people being led up that hill to the jungle camps where their captors would demand money in return for their release or safe transport over the border to Malaysia where they would hopefully find work and be reunited with family who had made a similar journey over. It was a miserable trek up and a quiet one down. Volunteers had already been up to the camp with its tarpaulin, makeshift tents and reminders of the people who once lived here—shoes, packets of chips, personal hygiene items. There were little flags around the graves that volunteers had begun to excavate. Authorities said some died of starvation or illness, others from what they referred to as violence. I thought of Srebrenica and the massacre there. The scale was different but our reason for doing our jobs was not. We were here in this Thai jungle camp to witness the evil that had taken place here and to tell the world what we were seeing and to shake the world and the authorities into action. I thought of my journalism heroine, Christiane Amanpour. I liked her in her days reporting in Bosnia. As a young child growing up just across the sea in Rome, Italy, in the early 1990s, I was exposed to images of Sarajevo and of the injured and dying. My linking these graves to Bosnia was also in part due to the fact that our photographer was from there. What was he thinking?

That day we trekked back down the hill, some of the Thai volunteers were chit chatting amongst themselves. My newly married husband, who was there filming for a competitor, and I and the rest of our pack were morose. Twenty-six bodies had been exhumed so far, most of them men but there was also a woman and one *unknown.*

In July 2017, a Thai court handed down guilty verdicts in what was being touted as the country's largest ever human trafficking trial. More than 100 suspects, including government officials and a Thai army general—had been accused of trafficking Rohingya Muslims from Myanmar and Bangladeshi nationals. The wave of arrests began after the discovery of the graves in 2015. I went to cover the trials a number of times and sat on the hard wooden benches trying to look for a reason in the eyes of those accused for why the guilty ones did what they'd done. I never did find one. But that July it felt like I had, at least with this story, and for a brief moment, come full circle. Three years later I was filmed for a look back piece to be screened at an award ceremony for the Society of Publishers in Asia (SOPA) and was asked why reporting about the ship landings and jungle camps mattered. I replied that once we saw the sentences handed down, that's when we realized that the reporting that we had done had actually been of some use and had put some of the perpetrators of these atrocities behind bars.

Today, as I write this, I am no longer a journalist. I left the profession just before having my second son to pursue a role in communications.

However, in my heart I will always be a reporter and people's stories and what brought them to each moment in their life or to a particular country or city will always fascinate me. My husband sometimes half jokes that I should mind my own business more and not ask every person they meet what their life story is. Did I become a *real* reporter? I hope so. I like to look back on those interviews in Takua Pa as a moment when things shifted and the stories those men recalled moved me and ignited a fascination that took me crisscrossing across southern Thailand for the next year.

There are those who think reporters are there to just document the story and should not be the story nor too emotionally involved. My view is that it should fall somewhere in between. That day on the hill along the Thai-Malaysian border I was many things: a reporter, a witness and a human being recording what other human beings and a person who could still not quite comprehend, why humans do to other humans the things that they do. Climbing down that hill in southern Thailand, it would have taken a herculean effort to not let those men in Takua Pa, the jungle camp and those shallow graves stay with me for the rest of my days.

Contributors

Seema Viswanathan is a journalist based in Kuala Lumpur, Malaysia, with twenty-five years of experience covering politics, business, fashion, beauty, travel, and social trends. In the past, she was the Editor-in-Chief of several women's glossies, including *Cleo, Female, Her World* and *Shape*. She is now a pen-for-hire, freelancing as a sub-editor, writer, and content consultant. In her free time, Seema indulges in her love of hiking, painting and reading.

Jervina Lao has covered various history-making events in Asia as a journalist with wire agencies *United Press International, Agencia Efe* and *Agence France Presse*. Later she joined Singapore's *The Straits Times* and then segued into digital news with MSN. She is currently based in Hong Kong where she works as a freelance writer and sub-editor. She also dabbles in fiction, with her short stories published in the Hong Kong Writer's Circle annual anthologies.

Amandra M. Megarani is a journalist for Tempo's weekly magazine, newspaper and website, from 2007 to 2017. She covers almost everything: from national economy to local elections, from city to lifestyle. She also writes features on arts and culture. Currently, she works as a content editor based in Jakarta, Indonesia for a global news aggregator. She spends her free time as a recreational runner and a history enthusiast. She is a mother of two (will be three).

Melizarani T. Selva is a Malaysian writer, journalist and spoken word poet, with notable performances at ZEE Jaipur Literature Festival and TEDxGateway. Her first book, *Taboo* is a poetic exploration of her Masters' thesis on the constructs and representations of the Malaysian Indian Identity. Her poems have been translated into French and Bahasa Malaysia. She reported for *New Straits Times* and *Star Media Group* in Kuala Lumpur before pivoting her career towards international marketing and the arts industry in Singapore. Presently, she serves as co-editor of the Singapore based literary magazine *SingPoWriMo.com*.

Zulaiha Anjalika Kamis Gunnulfsen is the Founder and Editor-In-Chief of *Fab! Luxe*, a digital lifestyle magazine. She has been a freelance journalist for more than a decade, contributing and penning her thoughts and sharing experiences on matters relating to lifestyle, image branding, yoga and wellbeing both on print and digital, internationally. Anjalika brings with her experience of more than 10 years in Marketing Communications, prior to travelling the world, living in various exciting cities around the globe. She currently divides her time between Kuala Lumpur, Malaysia and Singapore.

Nastasha Tupas is an Australian multi-platform journalist, reporting extensively across the military space, veterans' issues, cyber security, health, social issues and geopolitics in the Indo-Pacific. She is keen on human interest storytelling and has previously held roles as a Content Producer, Online Journalist, Digital Producer, Website Manager and Social Media Editor for a number of media companies in Australia, the US and the Philippines. Nastasha's written and video production work have been published online internationally after she began her career as a Video Producer which led to a short-term opportunity as a Digital News Presenter. In her free time, she likes to travel, work on her photography skills, do a bit of DIY furniture-flipping and she also enjoys hanging out at home with her cheeky little black cat, Sabrina.

Caitlin Liu is the managing editor of *Forkast.News*. Before that, she was a contributing writer for *Condé Nast* and a staff writer at the

Los Angeles Times, where she shared a staff Pulitzer Prize for breaking news. Her work has also appeared in *The New York Times* and The Washington Post.

Marissa Carruthers is an award-winning journalist who relocated to Cambodia in 2012 after working on newspapers in the UK for almost a decade. In Cambodia, she spent five years as editor of a lifestyle magazine and is currently a freelance journalist, contributing to *South China Morning Post, BBC Travel, TTG Asia, Mongabay* and other publications.

Reta Lee is currently working as an editor-in-chief for an online media brand and has previously written for many Malaysian, Singaporean and International publications. Her first foray in publishing began in 2006 after university, when she was writing for two entertainment magazines, *hot* and *HELLO!* in Malaysia, covering both lifestyle and entertainment beats (both magazines have since ceased). Then, she rode the digital wave in 2009 onwards, when she wrote for *MSN* and *Business Insider*. As an entertainment journalist by heart—she's interviewed everyone from Lady Gaga to James Marsden, Sophie Turner, John Lithgow and Susan Downey.

Valencia Tong is an award-winning writer and editor who specializes in contemporary art with a focus on the Asia-Pacific region and emerging markets. Her work has been published widely in print and online internationally. She is interested in a wide range of media, including drawings, paintings, illustrations, street art, video and media art, design and architecture. Currently, she explores the intersection between art and technology, such as virtual reality, augmented reality, artificial intelligence and blockchain, as well as the influence of music on art.

Although Journalism will always be her first love, **Ista Kyra** has since pivoted from writing about politics to documenting Malaysia's arts and culture scene. She runs Eksentrika, a community media that hosts an Artist Registry of talents in multiple countries in Asia, as well as stories and guides related to creative fields across disciplines. She has also been a marketing and consumer insights specialist since 2017. Prior, she was a journalist with *The Malaysian Insider*, *The New Straits Times* and *The Malay Mail*.

Susanah Cheok is an accomplished multi-platform publishing professional, who spent the last three decades shaping the consciousness of readers through precise and honest writing in Singapore's leading print magazines and websites such as *Her World*, *Female*, *Nuyou* and *Shape*. The founder of *The Edit*, a content creation consultancy, is an ardent advocate of kindness to animals and a devoted mother of four cats. Susanah Cheok contributes to various websites, including *curatedition.com*, KrisShop's *The Edit*, *Yahoo.sg* and *CNA Lifestyle*.

Ann Marie Chandy worked as a full-time journalist with the Star Media Group in Malaysia for close to three decades, working her way up from trainee to Deputy Executive Editor. She is currently editor for Malaysia's *Cultural Economy Development Agency (CENDANA)*. When she is not bingeing on television during her precious free time, she indulges in therapeutic art exploration and listening to music.

Lee MyIne is an award-winning freelance travel journalist based in Brisbane, Australia. She has been a regular contributor to the travel sections of *The Australian* and *The Telegraph* (UK) and the author of *Frommer's Australia* for more than a decade. She is a Life Member and former president of the Australian Society of Travel Writers.

Niki Bruce is an experienced media professional with more than twenty years in the industry, writing for print, online and social media in a wide range of genres covering everything from news to fashion. After thirty years in Asia, Niki has returned to Australia to impart her hard-won wisdom and cynicism to unsuspecting students and interns as a lecturer and the creative director of Revival Runway—a non-profit incorporated association dedicated to supporting independent Australian fashion brands and businesses and supporting students in the creative industries.

Jayagandi Jayaraj was a journalist with the Star Media Group for ten years, covering local news and lifestyle stories. She also had a gig with *Gulf Times* as a feature writer when living in Doha, Qatar. Upon her return to Malaysia, she served as the Deputy Editor of *Shape Malaysia* for several years under Blu Inc Media. She's still writing for various clients and exploring her options while indulging in her other passions; baking and crafting.

Erna Mahyuni is a columnist and sub-editor at *Malay Mail*, having started her career in tech journalism. From working with refugees at the UNHCR, reviewing games for IGN and the occasional foray into the performing arts, her varied interests help inform her sharp commentary on current affairs.

A multiple-award-winning journalist, **Zela Chin** started her career at CNN headquarters in the US and later joined CNN in Hong Kong. She now produces TV reports on social issues and business stories in the Asia region. She is the executive vice president of the Asia chapter of the Asian American Journalists Association, is on the Board of Governors of the Foreign Correspondents' Club, Hong Kong, leads the Duke University alumni association in Hong Kong, and sits on the board of the Duke Asian Alumni Alliance.

Muna Noor cut her teeth writing in the men's lifestyle space before a segue into writing for music, clubbing and street style magazines. During her fifteen-year career, she's managed a bumper crop of homegrown and international print and digital titles. Her passion is in conservation and travel, and in between volunteering for wildlife and nature NGOs and hiking, she regularly contributes freelance articles and writes from her blog *Pokok Kelapa*.

Ushar Daniele is an independent journalist based out of Kuala Lumpur. She specializes in current affairs and investigative storytelling in Malaysia and across the wider region. She reports for various news agencies and broadcasters including *Al Jazeera International, VICE News, CNN, South China Morning Post*.

Sher Maine Wong is a former Straits Times journalist and current freelance writer who considers it a life blessing that her passion for writing pays the bills and opens doors to people, experiences and first-hand knowledge which she would never otherwise have access to. She is now busy telling stories about people in HR and technology.

Amy Sawitta Lefevre was Reuters' Chief Correspondent and Deputy Bureau Chief for Thailand and Indochina where she covered political unrest, general elections, natural disasters and human trafficking. Amy has appeared on *CNN*, *BBC* and *Al Jazeera*, to name a few. She is a two-time recipient of the Society of Publishers in Asia (SOPA) award and a winner of the Human Rights Press Awards.

Acknowledgements

I would like to thank the late Mei Ann, my first editor, for seeing a spark in me and giving me a chance. Special thanks to my husband Benjamin Carle for kicking my ass and loving me at the same time.

Thanks to everyone who contributed and shared their experiences; I hope you'll cherish the time we worked on this book, as we now share a piece of history together.

Gratitude to the Penguin team, especially to Nora Nazerene, Associate Publisher, who is ever patient with me, sharing advice and your wealth of knowledge, and Amberdawn Manaois, editor, for your important inputs.